GRAM-O-RAMA

GRAM-O-RAMA

Breaking the Rules

Daphne Athas
Edited and with a Foreword by Marianne Gingher

iUniverse, Inc.
New York Lincoln Shanghai

GRAM-O-RAMA
Breaking the Rules

iUniverse books may be ordered through booksellers or by contacting:

iUniverse
2021 Pine Lake Road, Suite 100
Lincoln, NE 68512
www.iuniverse.com
1-800-Authors (1-800-288-4677)

Because of the dynamic nature of the Internet, any Web addresses
or links contained in this book may have changed
since publication and may no longer be valid.

ISBN: 978-0-595-44222-5 (pbk)
ISBN: 978-0-595-68850-0 (cloth)
ISBN: 978-0-595-88553-4 (ebk)

Printed in the United States of America

Contents

Gram-O-Rama Exercises

Foreword

Sometime during the mid-1970s, in the normally placid hallways of Greenlaw, which houses the English department at the University of North Carolina in Chapel Hill, I overheard buzz about a "language show" that was about to be performed by Daphne Athas's Stylistics class. Faculty and students alike hurried to claim seats in Donovan Lounge, and caught up in their enthusiasm, I joined an audience that quickly overflowed the room. People who hadn't gotten seats didn't leave; they gathered in large numbers, giddy with expectancy, around the walls. Something dramatically significant, perhaps historic, was about to happen on stage, and nobody wanted to miss it.

Without fanfare or preamble, in marched a troupe of players, brandishing scripts in black binders. They bowed in unison, then began to chant a rousing, rhythmically sophisticated fugue of nonsense that, the closer you listened, began to make a warbling kind of sense. The initial braiding of melodic and linguistic abstractions yielded to the clarity of emerging patterns and themes, like birdsong. You felt stirred by surprises of language, its bombast, delicate trills, and glissandos. Your spine hummed like a tuning fork. Your neck hairs stood up like tiny antennae lifted by the breeze of an enchanted medium, a kind of verbal helium. A circus of wordplay commenced. The performers punned and parodied, spoonerized, malapropped, alliterated, permutated sentences, conjugated verbs, clowned around with passive voice, tongue twisters, and faked foreign languages. They slid down the poles of consonants and bounced on the buoyant trampolines of vowels. They acted out comedy skits, spoken choruses, dialogues, and call-and-response dramatics. They musicalized speeches and conducted a symphony of kazoos. All skits were performed in maverick homage to the eight parts of speech, to the fundamentals of grammar.

Now, there's a dirty word for many students, my olden self included.

When I was a kid, I don't know which curricular activity struck the most dread in my heart: the study of grammar or arithmetic. They share a common synapse or two of left-brain logic, but as traditionally taught in public schools, they can zap the cheer out of a classroom faster than the cancellation of recess. Grammar, as it was taught to me, was anti-recess.

The teachers who taught it were stringent prune-faced sticklers, their classrooms filled with rows of electric chairs, not desks. If you forgot some ironclad rule of grammar, you fried, pal.

I watched the stylistics class's language show with fascination, not only because it was clever and entertaining, but because its grammar lessons were sleight-of-hand, and so fully integrated with spirited showmanship and fun that the mechanics of language and syntax disappeared into art. The show was antidotal to everyone's fear and loathing of grammar. The old rules had been outfitted with wings and this was what Grammar Heaven looked like.

During the 1970s, Daphne Athas, long-time lecturer in UNC's creative writing program and recipient of the university's 2003 Lifetime Mentoring Achievement Award, originated and developed a course she dubbed "Glossolalia." The word traditionally applies to religious sect members who speak an unintelligible rant when in the throes of spiritual ecstasy. Its Greek origin signifies "tongue chatter." In appropriating the term for her class, Athas meant to provide students with a no-holds-barred immersion in the ecstasies of language, its riptides of rhythms and sounds. The ultimate goal of the course was to revivify her students' appreciation for the flexibilities of language, the full spectrum of its communicative powers, from purest meanings to musical possibilities. Through a series of grammar-oriented exercises, she determined to turn the classroom into a multi-media laboratory where writing and oratory experiments would freshen respect for language as a fluid resource that was more than the sum of its phonemes and rules of engagement.

Under the rubric of "Stylistics" (47W), "Glossolalia" was launched as the quirkiest course in the creative writing program's sequence. It quickly achieved cult status on campus and has enjoyed an enduring influence on students who took it. Participants were delighted by the novel ways in which the serious study of grammar could be fused with wordplay, poetry, music, linguistic theory, literary history, and performance art. Interdisciplinary in scope, "Glossolalia" attracted students from the departments of drama, communication studies, music, as well as English and other liberal arts disciplines campus-wide. In the late 1970s, alumni of "Glossolalia" formed a private, nonprofit corporation and mounted a traveling production company, also called "Glossolalia." A team of actors introduced Athas's rollicking methodologies to public schools throughout the state. Meanwhile Athas continued to teach her college version of "Glossolalia" and produced a stylistics-related commentary for local Chapel Hill radio.

When Athas retired from full-time lectureship in the mid-1980s, she suspended teaching "Glossolalia," and focused on writing a textbook that would help to summarize and codify her theories regarding language's kinship with music. The resulting textbook, *Glossolalia: A Book of Language*, was, in part, a collection of the experimental exercises that had been performance successes of her Stylistics class. It was also a book about the development of language through the ages, and the influential writers who pushed the boundaries of convention to claim stylistic territories all their own (most notably, Gertrude Stein). It had the pragmatic aspects of most grammar books: rules and definitions and explanations of terms used. But it was an opinionated, often droll, and philosophical book as well. With its gutsy enthusiasms, its frequent diatribes against our TV saturated culture, its persuasive riffs on the influences that cosmic forces exert on language, *Glossolalia* played fast and loose with the standard buttoned-down erudition we've come to expect from textbooks. This was precisely why I was drawn to the book. It appealed to the child in me that had always agitated in the presence of prune-faced knowledge. *Glossolalia: A Book of Language* was something jolly other.

Nearly fifteen years passed, and Daphne Athas's hiatus from teaching "Glossolalia" appeared permanent. Former students often inquired about the status of the course, but the official weather report was that it was gone with the wind. She had formatted her textbook for public consumption but had yet to find a publisher.

In the fall of 2001, while serving as director of the creative writing program at UNC, I persuaded Athas to resurrect "Glossolalia." I offered to serve as her apprentice so that I could learn firsthand how she facilitated such a rambunctious academic experience. It seemed of paramount importance that the English department make provisions for preserving not only a course in stylistics but this provocative version in particular, with its content, vision, and methodologies intact. Athas accepted the challenge with characteristic enthusiasm. "I'm excited about doing it," she confided, as we geared up for the start of the semester. "Mainly because it's been so long since I've done it that it will be like making it up all afresh." This has long been her defining strength as a teacher—and an abiding gift to her students: she dotes on challenging herself to think "afresh."

Our class of eighteen guinea pigs crowded around a seminar table in a windowless room painted blank paper white. On the first day of class, Athas cajoled us into chanting each others' names with varying stresses to produce extemporaneous fugues. We talked about vowel and consonant sounds, diphthongs, fricative, and glottal pronunciations, nonreferential "beautiful" and "ugly" words. Someone suggested that "diphthong" sounded like an ugly word, and everybody laughed.

The first half of the semester was spent familiarizing ourselves with Athas's textbook, reading selections that had relevance to fifteen assigned exercises. Students wrote and orally delivered a writing assignment every class meeting, at "the pace of a steeplechase," Athas called it, cracking her licorice whip.

The second half of the semester we refined or revised the exercises previously written and selected those that were most promising in performance for inclusion in a language show. With patient collaborative effort that required frank criticisms and restrained egos, students decided upon a unifying theme and built a script of appropriate exercises around it. They rehearsed the exercises as skits, orations, chants, dialogues, poems, parodies, and musical numbers, and, at term's end, staged a language show that played to a lively, packed audience. "Glossolalia" was born again, and its rowdy phonological spectacle (a hybrid doubtlessly rooted in various influences including "Sesame Street," "Saturday Night Live," alternative rock, Pee Wee Herman, and poetry slams and improvisational theatre) proved to enthrall this newest generation. At this writing, the course approaches its sixth consecutive year as a regularly offered class.

What follows is an edited version of Daphne Athas's original book. It was not my intention to simplify the text or depersonalize it. One of the original book's most sparkling assets was the author's delightfully subjective treatment of a subject—grammar—that has spent so long moldering in other books designed for classroom use, that just the thought of opening such lifeless tomes releases warnings of toxicity in the user's brain.

I've attempted merely to streamline "Glossolalia," replace particular exercises with less dated material, clarify and tweak, and supply a glossary of useful terms. The glossary references the "greatest hits" from the more explicative text. It's possible that teachers wishing to use *Gram-O-Rama* as simply a resource for writing exercises will find supplementary information in the glossary that will facilitate understanding without further reading. But the serious reader will be shortchanged if he or she merely glosses. Having taught from the original textbook, I have done my best to preserve its integrity, quirks, insightfulness, and charm. I have tremendous respect for Athas's monumental achievement: that of making grammar not merely palatable or understandable, but wildly inspirational and—dare I say it—fun. Grammar as performable art? Who'd have thunk it possible? Only a maverick grammarian eager to share her lifetime's rapture for the written word and its everlasting music.

I am forever indebted to Daphne Athas for providing me the opportunity, both challenges and delights, of editing this gem of a book. Kudos to Bland Simpson, current director of the creative writing program, who gave the nod to this project and supported it in stellar ways, and to friends and colleagues who continue to jostle one another for front row seats at every stylistics performance and applaud and laugh and praise our jubilee. Thanks to our graduate assistant, Pamela Hamilton (now there's a poem of a name), for her patience and good cheer; to Greg Hohn of Transactors Improv for theatrical tips and assistance; to Daniel Wallace, for his jaunty art; to interns Matthew Spangler, Laurel Zmolek-Smith, Whitney Ward, and Jeff Fowler; and to the ongoing parade of Stylistics students who bedazzle and inspire us.

Marianne Gingher
The University of North Carolina at Chapel Hill
2007

Origins and Acknowledgements

This book is the outcome of many years of collaboration with students, colleagues, and friends. That it was generated in the creative writing program of the University of North Carolina at Chapel Hill is a testament to humanities education in an age of difficulty. There are so many people I want to thank that I'm hard put to be sure all their names appear here.

I am indebted to my colleague, Marianne Gingher, novelist, teacher, and former director of creative writing at UNC. She was a faculty member when I was asked to teach a course called Stylistics in 1976. She witnessed the eight year evolution of that class until 1984 when I cut down my teaching schedule. In 2001, after a fifteen-year hiatus, she suggested reinstating it and offered to co-teach it with me. Without her enthusiasm, team-teaching, and her adaptation and editing, the book would not have seen the light of day.

I recognized from the beginning that the word *stylistics* was a catch-all term for writing style and language. Many faculty members had taught the class with individual emphasis, so I knew I would have *carte-blanche*.

In the sixties, the National Council of Teachers of English abandoned the teaching of traditional grammar, which split the educational establishment and caused a schism between Grammar Ignorami and Grammar Nazis. Weak in traditional grammar, parts of speech, and diagramming, the average student claimed not to care. Most students also quit reading for pleasure. TV took its place, and the Internet was imminent. The privileged students who knew grammar (sort of) from Latin or private schools pretended it didn't count. The majority stuck to their fear and loathing, and everybody shared shame and guilt.

Much as I love grammar and reading, I had no wish to take on the system. Being a product of traditional teaching, I remembered as a college undergraduate playing pranks with a subversive boyfriend in boring classes. We passed notes to each other in fake German and Russian and after class swapped our guesses at meaning. World War II was going on. Being bookworms, we had learned without realizing to hear grammar. We'd become accustomed to the sound of music and mathematical balance in sentences. We'd come to believe that you couldn't think straight without it. Sure, words had reference, but logic demanded sound and rhythm for life, depth, and thrill. That's what gave authenticity. Wayne Williams, that friend, grew up to become the media director at UNC Greenville, and I thank him as the impetus behind this experiment.

I started the course with nouns. Jorge Luis Borges had invented hemispheres in his story, "Tlon, Uqbar and Orbis Tertius," where people had no nouns, and had to convey persons, places, or things with prepositional phrases, adjectives, interjections, or verbs. I gave the students this exercise. It produced some stunning metaphorical turns. I moved forward in the next class to verbs. Borges had appeared on William Buckley's *Firing Line*, extolling English for being a loose language. Verbs didn't need inflections if you wrote down one common verb and followed it with changes of prepositions in a series. Read on. Think up. Write down. You could say anything this way. You could create a plot, even a story. But verbs went beyond. They had different tenses, different moods, different voices. Why not describe flossing your teeth, or stuffing a turkey restricting yourself to passive voice? You might not know the difference before you've done it, but once you have, you can't get loose of it. What a revelation! One student changed into passive all the active verbs in Robert Frost's "The Road Not Taken."

I began thinking up exercises for the other parts of speech. Always they were designed on principles of distortion or restriction, a kind of language game. What was happening was that we were accessing grammar on the audio level by disturbing its function or rhythm in a sentence. We moved into figures of speech and common usages. The goal was to get the feeling and rhythm of possessives, participles, gerunds, collective nouns, infinitives, and misplaced modifiers as they functioned in a sentence. This led to drollery, nutty experiments in parody, fake languages, nonsense, puns, pure sound and rhythm, gibberish, and malapropisms. Halfway through the semester, it became obvious that for ultimate affect students would have to perform their work. They compiled a script of their best riffs and unified them by theme, character, or rhythmic sound continuity. The affect was immediate. Chris Potter and Jo Vanderford, students in the TV/Movie Department, borrowed cameras and filmed it.

The shows of following years ranged from didactic to symphonic. Rick Palmer, Tom Cox, and Andy Brawn in the Division of Instructional Technology entered into a second creative process. They directed and taped each new show as a studio production. A collection of these shows on VHS and DVD is held in the House Undergraduate Library's nonprint facility.

When I stopped teaching the class, I could not stop thinking about it, so I sat down to write and research. If the process of teaching had been an exercise in hearing grammar, the process of writing revealed the sources, which ranged from

Shakespeare and Swift to Gertrude Stein, Joyce, Vonnegut, Pinter, and the Beastie Boys, a canon of western literature, drama, and music. I called the book *Music and Pure Meaning*. This Platonic title betrays its idealism. But over the course of time I became increasingly convinced of the usefulness of the exercises for teaching. In games lie the seeds of new thinking, and in nonsense dwells the structure of grammar. The exercises are the meat and potatoes of the book. Student work comprises the illustrations. But I also included classical tables of conjugations, pronunciation, charts from old grammar texts, summaries of major laws and theories, and historical accounts of language evolution., for in spite of the ass-backward teaching method, I could not deny sources so redolent of Western history and American thought.

I showed the first draft to my friend, the late Wilton Mason, composer, writer, and former head of the department of music at UNC. He extolled the wrong-way grammar process for students who not only didn't read but also chose creative writing courses as their favored outlet to understand themselves. He wrote a six-page interlinear with stunning notations, and he corrected errors suggesting new ways of correlating language and music. One of the things he delightedly pointed out was that the Pythagorean scale, based on quavers of lyre strings at mathematical intervals, sounds horrible in real life.

Meanwhile, students from the first four classes organized a nonprofit corporation called Glossolalia, Inc. Mark Meares, afterward editor of the *Advocate* and the *Leader*, now director of corporate development for UNC-Chapel Hill; Linda Craven Kastleman; the late Jane Nunnellee; and Elizabeth Moose, teacher of English and creative writing at the North Carolina School for Math and Science, served as a board of directors. They won grants from the Z. Smith Reynolds Foundation and North Carolina Arts Council, and organized a cast of equity paid performers, Rob Worrell, Kathy Clarke, and Ralph Thompson, to take grammar shows and workshops throughout the state's elementary and high schools, and community colleges.

As alumni of the course distinguished themselves in their careers, they kept asking for updates on the book. Among these Stylistics alumni are children's writer Clay Carmichael, novelist Sharlene Baker, Southern Book Award Winner Randall Kenan, Professor-writer of the University of Colombia in South America Tim Keppel, mystery writer Katy Munger, and journalists Sharon Brody and Roger Wall. In the field of publishing, I thank Alane Mason, W. W. Norton editor and founder of the online magazine *Words Without Borders*, who contributed edits to an early draft; editor-writer Will Blythe, former editor at *Esquire* and author who published a condensed version of the text in the literary journal, *Black Warrior Review;* former Algonquin Books editor Marie Price, who contacted agents and editors for a gamebook version; Mary Jo Southern, former editor and sales manager at Houghton Mifflin, who organized a reunion of the two generations of Stylistics alumni in 2000; and senior editor Kathy Pories of Algonquin, who contributed valuable technical information. I thank alumni, now theater, TV, and movie writer-producers, actors, and editors Michael Cumpsty, Dave Krinsky, David Palmer, Virginia Hege, Mario Baldessari, and Suzanne Bolch. Jocelyn Neal, professor of music theory at UNC-CH, aided me in musical notation, and Daniel Wallace, professor of creative writing and novelist, contributed the cover art. I also thank Peggy Rabb, Ann Wilson, Duncan Smith, Vasile Sofinetti, the late Buddy Burniske, Dr. Lochrane Grant, Miranda Cambanis, Eric Darton, and Michael Parker for their support and encouragement.

I am indebted to the following: John Adler, Susan Batten Dalton, Kelli Lea Boyles, Jeff Brady, Sharon Jeanne Brody, Susan Campbell, Teresa Coleman Martin, Jami Grist Burns, Joel Chernoff, Tamara Hall, Priscilla Holbrook, Thomas Kakassy, Larry Kirkland, Meryl Kuznetsoff Porter, Jo Martin, Bruce McGuire, Rick Miller, Forsyth Michie Alexander, Paula Needle, Owen Page, Diana Rice, John Sasser, Carol Slechta, Sarah Park Stuart Rankin, Melanie Sumner-Marr, Ed Taylor, Heather Williams, Michael Van Hecke, Vicki Winslow Wolfinger, and Charles Worth.

Always aware of context, I can't help but remember my two grade school teachers and my freshman English teacher in high school, whose boundaries of directive teaching contributed beyond their life spans. Miss Curley (second grade) used to heave herself up and down the rows to teach phonics, hovering like a moo-cow over each pupil, her forefinger stabbing the 'P' on the page at the moment she shot forth her passion of plosive. Miss Bessie Parsons (fifth grade) introduced those rules of grammar, which Gertrude Stein said you could learn in two weeks and after that, what? And Miss Harris (high school) taught the eight parts of speech and made us chant conjugations of common verbs until they became so idiotic and hallucinating they exploded into red glares, which was when we knew without being able to articulate it that time really does secrete logic and give the clue to how we think.

The difference in grammar and language between the 1970s and the twenty-first century is demonstrable, not only because of technology but also because of world values and changes in speech patterns. Declarative sentences spoken in the last decade climb upward to the interrogative now as if reality were arguable.

Ventures into virtual reality have made reality problematical. The world has swung toward speech and away from the written, and there is a nostalgia for authenticity. The more we assume truth is truer in improvisation, the more we recede from reflection. Simultaneously, nostalgia for the certainty of *Mayberry* reappears. Retro is considered quaint and cool. These attitudes have modernized the latest Stylistics classes; the current shows are less thematic, less operatic, less collaborative in some ways. Performances are staged live, the technology is better, and the punchy results resemble *Saturday Night Live*. Everybody gets to be a ham.

I want to thank my parents: my father, a Greek immigrant with a foreign accent who got his higher education in America, and my mother, a New England Yankee, who went to a finishing school and learned Latin, German, French, and music. One day when I was nine, my father was standing shaving in the bathroom at the end of the hall, holding his single-blade razor up in the sunlight like an aegis. His chin was a beard of white lather. "Come eeean," he invited, an expression he used interchangeably with "Welcome." For the first time, I noticed he didn't talk like us. "That's the wrong way to say it," I informed him, and when he asked: "What is the right way?" I shortened my *i* and repeated as mercilessly as Miss Curley, "Ih Ih In." He copied my sound perfectly lifting his upper lip with a grimace. An astonishing thing happened. In that one syllable he lost all authority. The long *e*, which had always led him into his "uh" sound had been a mysterious corridor to a powerful kingdom, and now he was reduced to ordinariness. Fortunately, he relapsed. As an autocrat with authority, he used to regale us with the news that in Greek the verb was everything; it included attributes of noun, adjective, adverb, and preposition. "Action speaks louder than words," he used to say.

Our mother gave him a run for his money boasting about how she'd learned to be the best speller at the Cambridge School for Girls. She imitated her teachers while stitching a pongee dress on her electric sewing machine for my older sister. The word was "Constantinople." She regulated the engine's groan by nuancing the pressure of her foot on the pedal, making it rise at differing rates of speed to a whine or descend to a growl, the needle pouncing up or pounding down for the guillotine effect.

"C-O-N-con," she began. She enunciated each letter separately and repeated each syllable and gathered the length of pongee for the slaughter. The groan rose to middle C, the needle bit the cloth, and then the silence was deafening. "C-O-N S-T-A-N" she continued. We were slightly bored in the beginning, for the process seemed arduous, but as she increased the rhythm of letter, syllable, and synthesis, we got sucked in. Then came her final journey after Con, Stan, Ti, and Nope, a swelling crescendo to the syllable: "Pull." Four times the needle had slammed. Four stitches. Four syllables. We sat on the edges of our chairs, mouths shaped to her sounds, waiting as she sailed into port. "Pull!" she cried: "Con-Stan-Ti-Nope-*Pull*!" mimicking the scale: "Do re mi fa sol." The whole five syllables sailed from her mouth, complete, and the ship entered G major, the Sun. It could have been John Winthrop's shining Jerusalem. But Jerusalem has only four syllables. It was Constantinople, the Greek capital of the Eastern Roman Empire, in which "Pull" means "polis," the Greek word for "city" before it was degraded by Turks into the "bul" of "Istanbul." "Turks can't pronounce Polis," our father shouted triumphantly.

Pronunciation inevitably connects to grammar, and as it changes from decade to decade, it demands constant exploration. If grammar is the key to critical thinking, the idea of this book is the ratio of nonsense to sense. Hear it and you know it. And so I thank my parents, my students, colleagues, and friends who have spoken and made me hear.

Daphne Athas
Chapel Hill, North Carolina
2007

1. A Noun Is a Noun Is a Noun

A noun is the name of a person, place, thing, idea, or state of being.

Essence of a noun

When Gertrude Stein said, "A rose is a rose is a rose," she seemed to be presenting several conflicting ideas about the noun *rose*. First of all, you might infer that she was saying that it's silly to try to get at the essence of a rose since it is what it is, and what else is there to say about it after that? Maybe she starts repeating it to get at the mystery of it. She takes repeating seriously, predicating that if you repeat a word, its essence becomes clearer, more tangible, palpable, and distinct in your mind and senses.

Try repeating the word *rose* ad infinitum. Better still, try the word *butter*. If you repeat *butter* more than fifteen times, the beating of the *b* against your lips and the *t* against your teeth will make it become ridiculous. You will laugh. You will go zany, then you will go numb, and finally the word will disconnect from its meaning.

Imagine being in a foreign country where you don't know a single word. The first word you will need is the noun and then the verb. You will point. Someone will repeat the word *water* or *friend* or *hamburger*. By repetition, you will know how to ask for what you need.

Repetition is an attempt at reaching the essence of the noun. It's basic, a first step. But there is more to a noun than merely repeating a thing's name. How do we get to that essential?

Can we, for instance, talk about a boat, a lizard, Abraham Lincoln, or anger without using the names for them? Astonishingly enough, we can. A noun is like an ancient shellfish bearing its own meaning inside its own shell. It has traveled for centuries gathering layers, like moss, barnacles, or weeds, retaining its essence reshaped by the accumulation, changed in coloration.

From time immemorial writers have been trying to get at that essence. So have lovers, students, and storytellers, and all people who care about saying it right. A noun is a substantive that operates as the subject or object of a sentence. That is its role in the network of grammar. Grammar is the medium for relationships, and it can no more contain all the possibilities in a name than a name can represent all the possibilities of a person. A name can define or describe us, but it cannot *be* us.

Call our relationships with family, friend, peer, and society our grammar. Can we be summed up by that grammar? No. Our self is the living entity hidden behind the name we go by, ultimately uncapturable even though recognizable. It is the living essence behind the name of a thing that we yearn to catch. There are certain ways we can go about it. These ways involve other words: nouns, verbs, adjectives. They involve them in their operational relationships or grammar.

First we look at the proper name. Then we use adjectives and verbs to describe it. We deal in similes and metaphors. And we use the forms of verbs called verbals: participles, gerunds, and infinitives. It's like trying to surround a dolphin from a boat in the open sea. We do not wish to harpoon or even to photograph him; we merely want to strike the right note on the tuning fork to make him speak.

Proper name

Some of us dislike, are afraid of, or feel uncomfortable with our given names. But in fact, the American habit of instant familiarity by first name, or even by nickname, is not, as we like to think, a personalization. It is the opposite: a generalization by paradox, a category under which our true being can be hidden and thus remain uninterfered with. There are many more Bills than Williams. *William* has altitude, makes demands, reveals unknown accretions of history or of botany: William of Orange, William the Conqueror, Sweet William. *Bill* is instantly recognizable and instantly acceptable. But who is *William*?

There is more emphasis on naming in modern society than ever. The tag is the keystone to advertising. To the degree a tag attracts or repels, causes love or anger, trust or fear, the selling of a product or person can be considered successful.

Was Ivan terrible in essence, or did he become the "Terrible" because of his bloody deeds? Many of the historical elect are crowned in our memory by a tag. They are easier to remember that way: Oedipus Rex, Catherine the Great, Vladimir the Destroyer. In many cases, their proper name is crowned by a noun, in others by an adjective with the article *the*, making it be understood as a noun.

Games with Nouns, Proper or Not

Exercise 1: Crowned nouns

Make two lists.

1. Look in the dictionary or encyclopedia and find names of former kings, popes, or historical personages who were known by an attribute, crowned by a characteristic, such as *Popeye the Sailor Man.* Choose five and list them indicating whether their tag is a noun or an adjective understood as a noun.

Example:

Jack the Ripper—noun.

2. Choose five well-known contemporary public figures. Give them a title in the manner of the names above. Arrange the five in a list indicating whether their tag is a noun or an adjective understood as a noun.

Suggestion: The sequential order of your list will have a rhythm and implied meaning. When you have chosen your names, you may want to rearrange, according to some instinct or logic, for maximum affect. Such ordering is more a matter of feeling than of logic.

Thing, place: The no-noun challenge

So far we have been dealing with people rather than things. We have been giving people another name, another noun, or an attribute expressed in terms of an adjective. But can we do what Gertrude Stein says and express a thing without using a noun?

In imagining a language without nouns, we are altering reality. But in what way? The writer Jorge Luis Borges created an inventive prose style that questioned and stretched the objective and narrow truth of nouns, and that idea is revolutionary. If objects don't exist, then a person can create any number of noun conceptions, according to Borges. It's equivalent to a man blind from birth imagining colors.

Using verbs and adjectives as prime unit substitutions for nouns, a writer may equivocate the essence of a noun. Take the noun *moon.*

Examples:

Traditional: The moon rose above the river.

Verbal Construction: Upward beyond the onstreaming, it mooned.

Traditional: the moon

Adjectival Construction: Round airy on dark

Exercise 2: No-noun exercise

In English, in addition to straight adjectives, we have adjectival words that stem from verbs—verbals. Participles, both the past and present, are verbals that act as adjectives. And we have, of course, adjective phrases and adjective clauses, which contain nouns. In the following exercise, let us refrain from using nouns and verbs, but let us accept prepositions and participles. Also let us accept the other verbal that acts as a noun, the gerund.

1. Write the following nouns reconstituted by other means. You may use adjectives, verbs, participles, infinitives, articles, prepositions, conjunctions, and gerunds. But do not use nouns.

Examples:

Telephone: a) dialing ringing wiring; b) electronic ringing interrupteds; c) ring silent, ring silent

Mother: a) wise womanly watching of woeful toddlings; b) old warming of the nesting; c) warm soft, fertile, loving

1. mother
2. aborigine
3. stud
4. mermaid
5. sheik

2. Write the following sentences using the same no-noun rule as above.

Examples:

Humpty Dumpty sat on a wall: Ovalling egged sitting stone-henged. *A cat has nine lives*: Meow meow living nine.

1. Down will come baby, cradle and all.

2. A bird sang in a tree.

3. The witch flies on her broomstick.

4. The train pulls into the station.

2. The Physics of Verbs

A verb is a word to denote action or being.

Attitudes toward verbs

The verb has never incurred such extreme ambivalence of homage or disapproval as the noun. That is because it is kinetic. It is pure energy, and people respond to energy as moths to light. The verb either *acts* or *is*. We see action and being as proof of life. To *live* and to *be* are visible images of energy.

Think of the wordless motion we see every day on TV. The screen vibrates, automobiles chase, eyes gaze, mouths speak, people shoot. The fact of motion impresses, attracts, beguiles. Often we don't care *what* vibrates, *who* gazes, *what* is said, *who* shoots *whom*, for we worship energy. Movement satisfies as objects cannot. We see our destiny and think of ourselves in a process of motion. If we don't know what we are or what we ought to do, at least we feel that we *are* and *do*. We even *die*. The grammar of ourselves may exist without any other part of speech, but it has to have the verb. Without the verb, we cannot exist.

Possibilities of verbs

Utter a verb by itself. It immediately flies out like an arrow and takes wing. Saying a verb may be a command to feel, to sense, to experience. Or it may be an evocation. You don't feel obliged to burrow into its being, as you do with nouns, or strike the chord that will release its essence. You don't have to wind yourself around it or figure out the meaning behind it. The more unhinged the verb from its subject and object, the more authoritative and resonant it sounds.

Exercise 3: Lone verb dialogue

Choose two or three verbs, no more. Design or arrange them, using any conjugation, number, tense, or mood. Use no nouns and no subjects. Write a dialogue so that a meaning can be derived from it. You may use two or more characters. Stock situations are good for this exercise.

Example:

"The Sheriff's Dilemma"

>Sheriff: Go.
>Outlaw: Go?
>Sheriff: Go.
>Outlaw:———
>Sheriff: Should go.
>Outlaw:———
>Sheriff: Ought to go.
>Outlaw:———
>Sheriff: Must go!
>Outlaw: Draw!
>Sheriff: Draw?
>Outlaw: Draw!
>Sheriff draws and shoots outlaw.
>Sheriff: Shot! Go! Go! Go!
>Outlaw:———(Dies.)
>Sheriff: Gone.
>Deputy Sheriff appears.
>Deputy: Gone? Shot?
>Sheriff: Gone. Shot.
>Deputy: Shot?
>Sheriff: Gone. Shot.
>Deputy: Shot?
>Sheriff: Should have gone. Should have shot. Drew. Shot. Shot. Had to shoot. Had to be shot. Had to go. Did go. Went.
>Deputy: Shot. Gone.

Combinations with helping verbs

Although simple present and past may be expressed by a one-word verb, all other tenses require a helping verb. You show future by adding *will* or *shall*. You show present, past, and future perfect tenses with the helping verbs *have*, *had*, and *will* or *shall have*. You use a helping combination formed of the verb *to be* to show continuous action: "I *am* going, I *was* going, I *will be* going." And it takes helping verbs to make the passive voice where the subject is acted upon: "I *am* hit." "The paper *was* stolen." The helping verbs *should, would, may, might,* and *could* express different versions of such moods as the conditional or subjunctive. For better or worse, such distinctions are considered increasingly precious in English and are fading away. But for gradations of exact meaning, they are still necessary. The following is a list of all the possibilities a verb is capable of.

Aspects of a verb

Person: First, second, third
Number: Singular, plural
Tense: Present, past, future, present perfect, past perfect (pluperfect), future perfect
Voice: Active, passive
Moods: Indicative, subjunctive; progressive or continuous, emphatic, imperative
Types: Declarative, interrogative, imperative
Conditional helping verbs: Can, may, might, could, would, should
Obligation helping verbs: Must, ought to, have to

Verb synopsis

Principal parts: to take (infinitive), took (past tense), taken (past participle)

Indicative Present

		Active Voice	Passive Voice
Singular	1st person	I take	I am taken
	2nd person	You take	You are taken
	3rd person	He, she, it takes	He, she, it is taken
Plural		Active Voice	Passive Voice
	1st person	We take	We are taken
	2nd person	You take	You are taken
	3rd person	They take	They are taken

Indicative Past

		Active Voice	Passive Voice
Singular	1st person	I took	I was taken
	2nd person	You took	You were taken
	3rd person	He, she, it took	He, she, it were taken
Plural		Active Voice	Passive Voice
	1st person	We took	We were taken
	2nd person	You took	You were taken
	3rd person	They took	They were taken

Indicative Future

Singular		Active Voice	Passive Voice
	1st person	I shall take	I shall be taken
	2nd person	You will take	You will be taken
	3rd person	He, she, it will take	He, she, it will be taken
Plural		Active Voice	Passive Voice
	1st person	We shall take	We shall be taken
	2nd person		
	3rd person		

Indicative Present Perfect

Singular		Active Voice	Passive Voice
	1st person	I have taken	I have been taken
	2nd person		
	3rd person		
Plural		Active Voice	Passive Voice
	1st person	We have taken	We have been taken
	2nd person		
	3rd person		

Indicative Past Perfect (Pluperfect)

Singular		Active Voice	Passive Voice
	1st person	I had taken	I had been taken
	2nd person		
	3rd person		
Plural		Active Voice	Passive Voice
	1st person	We had taken	We had been taken
	2nd person		
	3rd person		

Indicative Future Perfect

Singular		Active Voice	Passive Voice
	1st person	I shall have taken	I shall have been taken
	2nd person	You will have taken	You will have been taken
	3rd person	He will have taken	He will have been taken
Plural		Active Voice	Passive Voice
	1st person	We shall have taken	We shall have been taken
	2nd person	You will have taken	You will have been taken
	3rd person	They will have taken	They will have been taken

Subjunctive Present Singular

Singular		Active Voice	Passive Voice
	1st person	If I take	If I be taken
	2nd person	if you take	If you be taken
	3rd person	If he take	If he be taken
Plural		Active Voice	Passive Voice
	1st person	If we take	If we be taken
	2nd person		
	3rd person		

Subjunctive Past

Singular		Active Voice	Passive Voice
	1st person	If I took	If I were taken
	2nd person		
	3rd person		
Plural		Active Voice	Passive Voice
	1st person	If we took	If we were taken
	2nd person		
	3rd person		

Subjunctive Present Perfect

		Active Voice	Passive Voice
Singular	1st person	If I have taken	If I have been taken
	2nd person	If you have taken	If you have been taken
	3rd person	If he had taken	If he had been taken
Plural	1st person	Active Voice If we have taken	Passive Voice If we have been taken
	2nd person		
	3rd person		

Subjunctive Past Perfect

Same as the Past Perfect of the indicative

Subjunctive Future Perfect

		Active Voice	Passive Voice
Singular	1st person	If I were to have taken	If I were to have been taken
	2nd person		
	3rd person		
Plural	1st person	Active Voice If we were to have taken	Passive Voice If we were to have been taken
	2nd person		
	3rd person		

Imperative:

Take

Present Infinitive

Active Voice	Passive Voice
To take	To be taken

Perfect (Past)

Active Voice	Passive Voice
To have taken	To have been taken

Present Gerund

Active Voice	Passive Voice
Taking	Being Taken

Perfect (Past) Gerund

Active Voice	Passive Voice
Having taken	Having been taken

Present Participle

Active Voice	Passive Voice
Taking	Being taken

Past Participle

Active Voice	Passive Voice
Taken	Been taken

Perfect Participle

Active Voice	Passive Voice
Having taken	Having been taken

Indicative Present Progressive

Active Voice	Passive Voice
I am taking	I am being taken

Subjunctive Present Progressive

Active Voice	Passive Voice
If I be taking	If I am being taken

Indicative Past Progressive

Active Voice	Passive Voice
I was taking	I was being taken

Subjunctive Past Progressive

If I were taking

Present Emphatic

I do take, etc.

Past Emphatic

I did take, etc.

Exercise 4: Subject-verb monologue, dialogue, or chorus

Choose two or three verbs. Then either:

A. Create a soliloquy or monologue limiting yourself to the subject and different variations of the verb. If you need, use an object, or an adverbial conjunction as in the first illustration below, but limitation will produce the most interesting result.

or

B. Create two or three characters or groups of characters speaking to each other or against each other. You may have them argue in the manner of town meetings, strikes, or demonstrations. Limit yourself to subject and verb, although you may use the odd conjunction or two, and an infinitive if you need it. See the examples below. This exercise can reveal people's attitudes toward certain subjects: sales-men, seductions, sanctions, or soliloquies of the silenced. If the abstracted conjugations don't match, think of a specific situation and specific characters.

Examples:

The first illustration contrasts the conditional and subjunctive moods with the declarative and emphatic forms.

"I Couldn't and I Wouldn't," by Ann Wilson

> Oh, I hadn't
> And I didn't
> And I haven't
> And I won't
> 'Cause I couldn't
> And I shouldn't
> And I don't;

I had not
And I have not
I did not
And I don't
I will not
And I shall not
'Cause I shouldn't
And I won't.

"Die-Stop," by Priscilla Holbrook

He: Do you want to die?
She: I want to stop. I want to stop wanting. Is that dying?
He: You have to stop.
She: I can't stop. If I were to stop, I'd die.
He: You could stop wanting.
She: But I don't want to die.
He: You just want to stop?
She: Yes. Stop. But not die.
He: You can.
She: Can I?
He: Do you want to?
She: I can't stop wanting.
He: You'll stop wanting when you die.
She: Die? Then, I want to die.
He: No, just stop. You need to stop. Everyone needs to stop. It's not dying. It's just stopping.

Combinations with prepositions

Above all, a stunning achievement of English verbs can be demonstrated when you combine them with prepositions. English is a loose language that is at the same time extremely clear.

For instance, you can make a story with nothing but verbs by adding different prepositions. Common verbs like take, put, make, come, and get offer the widest variety of different meanings. But even with uncommon verbs you can get a progression of action that tells a story.

Another variation of this is to use a preposition before a verb. For example: the verb take. Use the preposition under as a prefix, and you get undertake.

Undertake has implications of something difficult, a job, a burden, and when you turn it into the noun undertaking, it grows even more serious, until the person who does it becomes an undertaker, the person who deals with the corpse in death. Use the preposition under after the verb, and you get take under, as in the expression "take under consideration." This presents an entirely different connotation.

The following two exercises are a call to practice the strength of a verb in its more unfettered state. The degree and variety of moods that a verb can express without its subject or object are astonishing.

If you do exercise three thinking of a particular action, that action may or may not be identifiable. But in many cases, it will have overtones: it will break through the particular toward the cosmic. Good poetry does this.

In both exercises, examples are given less as guides than as tuning forks to strike chords in your imagination.

Exercise 5: Loose verb story

Choose three or four common verbs. Add a preposition after each. Make a series that forms a plot. Use no other part of speech except the verb and its preposition. Title the piece. From your series we should have a general idea of what is happening without your having to designate subjects or objects.

The three following examples are representative of three very concrete actions, but you do not by any means have to stick to such mundane subject matter. Be as poetic or cosmic as you please.

Examples:

"Timber"
Look.
Look at.
Mark off.
Look at.
Mark off.
Chop.
Look at.
Mark off.
Chop in.

Saw through.
Saw through.
Saw through.
Saw through.
Saw through.
Saw through.
Saw through.
Look up.
Step back.

"Pumping Iron"

Suck in.
Puff up.
Strut across.
Show off.
Gross out.

Exercise 6: Stay loose, change plot

Choose one common verb. Write two different stories using only that verb—but change the prepositions. In effect, you may be telling the same story with two opposing outcomes or two different viewpoints. The difference will depend on the prepositions. Title each story. That will give the clue to the difference.

Example:

"The Good Night"   "The Bad Night"

By Jane Nunnellee

Turn in.   Turn in.
Turn over.   Turn down.
Turn to.   Turn over.
Turn on.   Turn away.

3. The Diminished Verb

Popularity of the verb: The implications

The strength of the verb has advantages and disadvantages. There have been two major trends that have changed and threatened language. The first is the nominalizing of the verb, making it material and categorical. (Example: That book was a good read.) The second is the use of the passive voice for deliberate obfuscation. (Example: The truth was softened by me.)

Changing Nouns to Verbs

Here are some examples of verbs made out of nouns: to atomize, to table, to chair, to motorize. Most words with -ize endings are such verbs. A way of summing up this paragraph would be to say: "The idea of making a noun into a verb is to scientize the verb."

You can recognize the nominalized verb in income-tax reports, government manuals, and sociology textbooks. Football players, doctors, boxers, educators, and ordinary people start talking this way whenever they are put into the limelight in street interviews or TV talk shows. It is the language of objectification.

Most people think of the process as verbing a noun rather than nouning a verb. The energy of a verb is always weakened by this transformation or "hybridizing."

When a noun is concrete, it ties the verb to matter, like tying a stone to the leg of a gull. It will fly, but not well. When the noun is abstract, the verb may become a fallacy carrier. Compare the following sentences to understand that energy of verbs is being maneuvered to form nouns and to obscure clear meaning:

A. The water rushes down in a thin sheet of glass.

B. Glass symbolizes water.

A. She smelled the steaming lobster before she ate it.

B. Steam atomized elements of water in the lobster; sensory odors were utilized and the girl's mouth salivated before her chewing was activated.

Not only have verbs been reduced to statics, but the noun as subject has also been reduced, even when the verb is active.

We can see the false direction. Verbs have been harnessed into nouns in the name of an objective truth. But the truth is lost, and the only way to get it back is to return to the nominal as subject. Simple verbs like halt, cross, swim, am, put, weep, take, shudder, shove, pray, or jump demand a subject because they have no trace of noun elements within themselves. Most of them cannot even take an object. And certainly they cannot render an abstract truth by logical extension.

The Passive Voice

There is one valid use of the passive voice. It is when the focus is on the person or thing receiving an action. In the sentence: "Brenda and Romeo were married by Reverend Rogers," it is Brenda and Romeo who are important, not Reverend Rogers.

But in most cases, the use of the passive voice is the ultimate objectification. It directly changes the subject into an object, and it conceals and may even bury the doer and receiver.

The goal of the passive is objectification. The result is often evasion, obscurantism, or deliberate confusion, ambiguity, and absurdity.

Exercise 7: The famous and the familiar passive switch

Take a famous passage from religious or political literature, a recognizable song lyric, poem, or nursery rhyme, or a paragraph of action from a short story or novel, and rewrite it, changing all verbs into the passive voice.

Example:

"The Road That Was Not Taken"
from the Robert Frost poem, rewritten by Annette Overton

> There was a divergence of two roads in a yellow wood,
> And sorrow was had by me that both could not be traveled by me
> And since one traveler was what I was, there was a long time that standing was done by me
> And one was looked down by me as far as looking-down could be done by me
> To where bending was what was done by the undergrowth.

Exercise 8: Official passive

Write a detailed account of a crime, atrocity, vice, felony, or misdemeanor using passive voice in the manner of a government report or defense-law brief. Think of the language of Nixon when he told the nation about the erased tapes. Or think of a child when he is explaining the pie that has disappeared from the windowsill.

Examples:

"Clam Chowder"

> On the night of January thirtieth, in an obscure darkened kitchen on the northern side of the state, a can was opened, at approximately 7:06 p.m. eastern standard time. Campbell's Manhattan Clam Chowder, age forty. Its contents were dumped into a nearby saucepan. The deed's perpetrator is not known at present, though it has been discovered by our sources that the contents were stirred, and heat applied. There seems to be some evidence that water was stirred in with the contents, which were then placed under cover. Suspicions have been confirmed by the lab report detailing "that the contents were removed from the source of the heat, and were poured into an earthenware receptacle. A spoon of unidentified base metal was utilized in the penetration of the contents' surface, and in the lifting out of a portion. The portion was tested, was found to be not in excess, and was returned to the receptacle. A tongue was burned in the process. The portions by which passage to the esophagus was found possible were digested, following a prescribed interim. It has been determined that digestion of the receptacle's entire contents was completed.

"Case History #22, Ms. Muffet"

> Ms. Muffet, Caucasian juvenile, aged twelve, was reported recumbent on a tuffet while milk heterogenized by the controlled introduction of rennet was being ingested by mouth. She was approached by a large arachnid alleged to be halted on a neighboring tuffet proximal to her posterior. A fright/flight reaction was induced in Ms. Muffet by alleged arachnid's proximity and the dilemma was resolved by an instantaneous movement of fleeing, accompanied by screams of "Mee Mee," and the appearance of wet spots answering the description of milk, curds, or whey.

Exercise 9: Passive satire

Write in the passive voice a sketch of such a fundamental action as a fashion show, the killing, dressing, preparation, and cooking of Thanksgiving turkey, taking a girl to a movie, or flossing your teeth. The action you choose should be basic and physical so that making objects of subjects will show up as ludicrous. The more varied you make your subjects, the more absurd your account will be.

Examples:

"Invalid Aunt," by Chris Simens

> Out of bed my body was lifted. My shirt was found folded over the chair and was pulled down over my head. Its collar was straightened and then my hair was combed. My pants were found and pulled up my legs and zipped and buttoned.
> I was hurried out of the room so that my invalid aunt could be taken care of by me.

"Passive Date, Wendy and Jim," by Sharlene Baker

> Wendy was stood next to by Jim. His sweaty palms were wiped on the legs of his pants.
> "Uh, Wendy … uh, what will be done by you tomorrow night?"
> "It is not sure yet."
> "It was hoped by me that a dinner could have been had and a show could have been gone to by us."
> "Now that it is thought about, I will be busy."
> "Oh, are plans had by you for Saturday night, too? It was thought by me that maybe the late show at the Varsity could be caught by us."
> "A comparison between Mark Twain and Edgar Allen Poe must be written by me Saturday night."
> Her tight, blue-striped sweater was impulsively looked at by him. He was caught. His tennis shoes were quickly looked down at by him.
> "Your type of guy is known by me; your rotten guts are hated by me. That big black Impala and its big back seat can be taken and shoven by you!"
> He was stormed away from by her.

"Auto Accident," by Jessica Luginbuhl
Dramatic Skit for 4 speakers (Man, Woman, Policeman, Bystander)

> Woman: My car was hit by you!
> Man: The fault was had by you.
> Woman: Mister, my car was hit by you.
> Man: It was hoped by me that late for work I would not be, and yet standing next to you is where I find myself, my car totaled by you and by erratic driving tendencies that are had by you.
> Policeman (entering): There is a problem here had by you both?
> Woman: My car was hit by him!
> Man: A lie is being told! The accident was caused by her!
> Policeman: Help can be given if quiet is had.
> Innocent Bystander (entering scene): Ahem! Could attention be paid to me by you? The accident was seen by me.
> Woman: My car was hit by him, right?
> Bystander: Woman, delusions are being had by you. His car was clearly hit by you.
> Policeman: Lady, the bystander is believed.
> Woman: Terrified is being felt by me; collapsing will be done by me; money is not had by me!
> Policeman: A court date will be set by us. In the meantime, crying must be stopped.

Subject or object

In the English convention of the sentence, an object demands a transitive verb and a subject to do the doing to it. A subject can, by means of a transitive verb, do something to an object, but if it has an intransitive verb it can simply *do*: for it does not demand an object as object demands a subject. The one great verb in the English language is called the verb *to be*. It is called the *copula*. It is different from other verbs because its predicate is the same thing as its subject. Shakespeare put in on the map with his famous line from *Hamlet*, "To be or not to be …" In taking no object, the verb *to be* is its own declaration, unadorned. Nothing more can be said, perhaps because nothing more is known. Furthermore, to be can elicit only relative pronouns or adverbs: *who, where, how,* and *why?*

To exist, of course, does not mean *to be*. It is alike, however, in that it cannot take an object. It may mean to merely exist and not to be. To have no essence, but to live, like a one-celled protozoan. But in any case, these substantive verbs of being, appearance, or essence, (*to be, to exist, to seem, to appear*) are mysterious. They are inclusive to the degree that they are without the possibility of logical progression. They can be neither expanded nor reduced. They are capable of infinite variation, refinement, and qualification, but they cannot be the x or y of any equation that is not circular.

The verb most similar to them is intransitive, the verb that does not take an object—"I think, therefore I am." We have arrived at pure essence by the route of the intransitive verb.

Let us consider intransitive verbs: *I think. I pray. I sit. I laugh.* You may think thoughts, pray a prayer, or laugh a laugh. Do you sit a seat? None of them is very good grammar. No, you cannot think, pray, sit, or laugh anything outside what the verb decrees. So, next to the substantive verb that gives its subject star billing and whose predicate is always a complement to that subject, only the intransitive verb so elevates its subject. There can be no confusion of subject and object when you are dealing with the intransitive.

The purpose of the next exercise is to practice your recognition of subject. There is no right or wrong answer. The best way to approach it is by impulse or instinct, off the top of your head. That noun that seems most natural to you as a subject lurks unspoken in your psyche. It is larger than language structure allows. Yet the tradition of the simple sentence waits. It is a medium, and it is available. It is still possible that it can be the catalyst to bring you to a recognition of the nouns you have always known to be subject rather than object.

Exercise 10: Subject or object

1. Name five subjects.

2. Name five objects.

3. Use the subjects in three sentences each. Can your subject be used as object? Write three more sentences in which your subject acts as object in the sentence.

4. Use the objects in three sentences each. Can your object be used as subject? Write three more sentences in which your object becomes the subject of the sentence.

4. The Complete Sentence in Two Parts

A sentence is a series of words forming the grammatically complete expression of a single thought.

The Union of Noun and Verb

Up to now we have dealt with nouns and verbs in their singularity. We have defined their roles without regard to their relationship with other parts of speech. Our assumption has been that the single word is an ideal universe and that the structure that connects it with others is relative.

In the sentence as structure, the ideal of completeness is based on the assumption that if an action (verb) exists, it must have a doer (noun). These are the two basic parts of speech. Let us consider the sentence as the center of gravity of the English language, as the stage or arena upon which the noun and the verb perform their drama.

Modifying structures

But if all sentences were limited to a main clause, language would be boring. Completeness would follow completeness. We would talk the baby language of "I Tarzan, You Jane," and the simple sentence would confront us with limitation and outright lie. For as humans, we have discrimination: we have the talent of complication, weight, and balance and nuance. The subjects and objects and the verbs of our sentence demand qualifications that change their meaning in context either radically or subtly. The two structural formations in language that perform these qualifications are the clause and the phrase. Both modify. Both are important. And both imitate the basic structure of the sentence in being composed of two parts of speech: the noun and the verb.

The Modifying Clause

The modifying clause is an imitation of the sentence. The only difference is that it does not stand alone. It is not complete. It needs a relative pronoun or relative adverb or conjunction, for it is a modifier. That is its purpose. It describes either the main verb of the sentence, or the subject or object. It is dependent.

However, this **subordinate, dependent clause** must, like the main clause of the sentence, have a subject and a verb. That's what makes it a clause. It conducts the same drama of substantive (noun) and verb as the main sentence clause, and it is made up of the same opposite and complementary elements of two: the noun and the verb. It is a mini-version or mirror image of the sentence, its purpose differing in that it modifies something in the sentence rather than standing on its own.

If the sentence is describing wholeness, its modifying clause's role is distinction, clarification, qualification. Example of a dependent clause in its relationship to the whole sentence:

I ate a roll that had poppy seeds on top. ("That" is the noun/pronoun/subject component; "had" is the verb component; the clause is dependent because it describes or quantifies the type of roll the narrator ate.)

The phrase

The phrase, although composed of at least two grammatically linked words, is not a mirror image of the sentence. It has no need of a verb. But it does deal with the idea of the noun as object, and the word that conveys objecthood is the preposition. The preposition (think pre-position) indicates the position of the object: near, under, over, by, around, to, from, etc.

A **preposition** is a word for relationship. The difference is not, as in the clause, between the thing (noun) and the action (verb), but between the thing (noun) and that which gives it its objecthood (preposition). This is a more illusive concept. The preposition denotes the whereness, howness, even whyness of the object.

Sometimes, instead of a preposition, a phrase has a **verbal** for its word of relationship. But the phrase's noun matter is always bound into objecthood, for its objectifier, whether it be a preposition or a verbal, is basically static compared with a verb.

How important is the prepositional phrase? It is as important as varied shades of red compared to the larger difference between red and blue. Qualitatively the distinction is extremely subtle, and there are many times it is better to avoid phrases.

Yet the phrase is the vehicle of subtle distinction, of complication. It must be respected.

Examples:

Prepositional phrase:
(**noun**) *Out of trouble* is where I want to stay!
(**adjective**) This is the mystery novel *with the last page gone.*

(**adverb**) She kissed her boyfriend *without enthusiasm.*

Phrases using verbals:
(**infinitive**) Not knowing *what to do*, she laughed.
(**gerund**) The nurse chided him for *sitting on the bed.*

(**participle**) *Listening to her complaints*, he cringed.

Varieties of the Sentence

Sentences vary as to type, order, and emphasis, and it is the positioning of clauses and phrases that defines this variety.

Types of Sentences

Simple. A simple sentence is made up of one main clause.

> **Example:** Your mother can't deal with it.

Compound. A compound sentence has two or more main clauses joined by a subordinate conjunction, a semicolon, or a comma.

> **Example:** Your father is proud of you and so am I.

Complex. A complex sentence has one main clause and one or more subordinate clauses.

> **Example:** Don't get in a car with a stranger because he'll take you away and make you do all kinds of nasty things like washing his clothes and cooking his meals and sweeping his floors.

Compound-Complex. A compound-complex sentence is a combination of the compound and complex, in that it has two or more main and independent clauses and one or more subordinate clauses.

Example: I drew this picture of her and when I finished, I drew in big block letters underneath: "I hate you, Mama."

Order

Standard. The standard order of a sentence in English is: (1) for intransitive verbs: the subject second; (2) for transitive verbs: the subject first, the verb second, the object third.

Example: You know we love you. (S, V, O)

Inverted. When you reverse the standard order of subject, verb, object to achieve a different emphasis, the result is called an inversion. Typical inverted sentences have such varied orders as (1) subject, object, verb; (2) object, verb, subject; or (3) verb, object, subject.

Examples: We love you, you know. (O, S, V)
How do I know it? (S, V, O)
Standard: Love can explain nothing. (S, V, O)
Inverted: There is nothing love can explain. (V, S, O)

Interruption. When you interrupt the normal progression of a sentence with a parenthetical expression or a long modifier, the result is called interruption.

Example: Lisa, my sister, whom I love, rode in the car.

Loose. A sentence is called loose when it ends with one or more elements, usually modifiers, which are not essential to the completion of meaning of the main clause. The longer these end elements are, the looser the structure becomes.

Example: I was seven years old before I knew my brother's name was John and not Bill because we had this toy telephone so Mom would say: "We're going to call Johnny, we're going to call Johnny," and she would dial a number and say: "Hello, Johnny," and then she'd say: "Say hello to Johnny, David," and I'd say: "Hello, Bill."

Periodic. When the meaning of the main clause is not completed until the end of the sentence, you have a periodic sentence. The longer the elements, the more marked is the periodicity. Inversion and interruption are typical methods of achieving the suspense incurred in a periodic sentence.

Example: With her thick brown hair falling onto her shoulders, each strand in place, with her eyes wide and greenish-grey, her uncompromising gaze steady and sharp through the steamy windshield, Lisa was disconcerting.

Emphasis

Parallelism. Parallelism is the repetition of similar grammatical structures for the sake of coherence or emphasis. The repeated structures may be large ones such as clauses, smaller such as phrases, or even key words.

> **Example:** Hang up the phone, dial 125, and ask operator 391 to connect you with the Santo Domingo exchange.

Balance. When the parallel components are similar in rhythm as well as structure, the result is balance.

> **Example:** She was outside on the fifth floor or the fourth floor; I was on the first floor or the ground floor; I don't know whether to call the first floor the first floor or the ground floor.

Antithesis: Parallel elements that contrast with each other result in antithesis in a sentence.

> **Example:** I always thought movies showed real people with real lives, but David thought they were two-dimensional celluloid figures with two-dimensional celluloid lives.

Gradation. When parallel components are arranged in a descending or ascending order of importance, the result is called gradation.

> **Example:** The car stopped; I remembered what David had said in Washington about the fan belt, got to the side of the road, pulled the brake, and sat there in the dark; I knew I had to telephone somebody, I got out with cars whizzing past, and I started walking back to the last exit.

Exercise 11: Types of sentences

Write a story, dialogue, anecdote, or stand-up comedy routine in the series of sentences listed below. Stick to the order and type of sentence.

Simple
Compound
Complex
Standard order

Inverted order
Interrupted
Loose
Periodic
Parallelism
Balance
Antithesis
Gradation

If you write a plot, make it say something or tell something. The cumulative affect of the sentences may express humor, surprise, amusement, or astonishment. Absurd juxtapositions contribute to humor. For example, Woody Allen takes an intrinsically absurd situation, gimmick, or framework, and uses vivid, concrete images to get his effect.

If you write a dialogue, listen to the sound of overtones or undertones. The most specific content may express the most profound thematic unity.

Examples:

"Tales of a World-Weary Space Cadet," by James O'Boyle

> **Simple:** Vince was a cosmonaut.
> **Compound:** He strapped on his superpack and he blasted off.
> **Complex:** Vince's kid brother always wanted to come along, but Vince told him that Bucky was no name for a cosmonaut.
> **Standard:** Bucky got mad at Vince.
> **Inverted:** To console himself he read science fiction novels and cried and cried and cried.
> **Interruption:** Bucky's life, when he came across a book called Tales of a World-Weary Cosmonaut, the story of Bucky Buckman, a boy who is bullied in grade school and rises to become the greatest cosmonaut in the universe, took a turn for the stupendous.
> **Loose:** When he had finished reading the novel, Bucky realized that his dreams could come true, that he could strap on his very own superpack and blast into space, that he could single-handedly save galaxies from imminent doom, that he could have thousands of beautiful cosmonaut babies with his beautiful cosmonaut girlfriend and endorse all kinds of spectacular cosmonaut products, all the while saying proudly: "I am Bucky, the greatest cosmonaut that ever was."

Periodic: Bucky, having found the strength he needed to believe in himself, having built his own superpack, the best one ever, because of Bucky's name in Day-Glo letters proudly painted on the back of it, and having added some atomic side-jets to the pack, pushed off.

Parallel: Bucky bucked his way to the top of the cosmonaut food chain; Bucky had balls; Bucky had the biggest balls in the universe.

Balanced: While in outerspace, Bucky saw many kinds of new plants: plants that could inspire poetry, plants that could throw great parties, plants that could have great conversations, and plants that could get a lot of girls.

Antithesis: Bucky loved the idea of being a cosmonaut, but he began to love the idea of being a botanist even more.

Gradation: In the end, Bucky realized something big: he realized that he had to do what made him happy; he realized that if he could become the greatest cosmonaut that ever was, then he could make a damn fine botanist.

"Stop, Thief!" by Eugeniya Bakunova

Simple: We stole a book.

Compound: I threw it over the detector and Misha caught it.

Complex: We stole it because it costs $211 in the bookstore and we both needed it for class.

Standard order: We felt guilty about it.

Inverted order: How we were going to share it, we had no idea.

Interrupted: Misha put our book, the stolen one, which neither of us wanted, into my backpack.

Loose: I pointed out to Misha that he was also involved in the theft and that he could not just say he did not want this stupid book and give it to me because I did not want it either and I had the same right to shove it into his backpack as he has to shove it into mine.

Periodic: Though Misha listened, carefully studying the space behind my head and not once looking at the backpack which I still refused to pick up, he did not hear a word.

Parallelism: The door opened, the cashier came out, the door closed, and the cashier approached me from behind.

Balance: The cashier called the policeman and the policeman arrested me; the policeman called the judge and the judge put me in jail; the judge called Misha and Misha gave him a bribe.

Antithesis: I told Misha that he was a dishonest treacherous thief who stole more than just one book, and Misha told me that I was an honest gullible thief who stole less than just one book.

Gradation: The court decided to forgive me my first offense; I stole all of Misha's stolen things; I gave half of them back to their previous owners; Misha bribed the judge $224, which is thirty-four cents more than what he would have paid for the book with tax; in the end I took pity upon Misha and compensated him for the thirty-four cents.

5. The Verb Unbound

Verbals

But what if the sentence is not the natural center of gravity for our thought?

In the *Oxford English Dictionary*, the first five definitions of "sentence" stress opinion and judgment:

> 1. Way of thinking, opinion … 2. The opinion pronounced by one person on some particular question, usually one on which he is consulted or which is being deliberated upon … 3. An authoritative decision, a judgment pronounced by a tribunal … 4. A quoted saying of some eminent person, an apophthegm … 5. An indefinite portion of a discourse or writing: a "passage" …

It is only by the sixth definition that we get the common grammatical definition: "6. A series of words in connected speech or writing, forming the grammatically complete expression of a single thought: in popular use often such a portion of composition or utterance as extends from one full stop to another."

Even as she strove to express the whole, Gertrude Stein hated completion. That was why she spurned nouns, seeing them as final in themselves, summed up, and lacking the vibrant present. She wanted the living/breathing of language, and because her education was philosophical and scientific—she studied philosophy at Harvard with William James and went to medical school at Johns Hopkins—she conceived of writing as *description*. How could you describe the living/breathingness of people? Working in a hospital as an intern, she noticed the differences between how people talked and how sentences were formed. Workmen, housewives, black people, and children spoke in a variety of partial structures, words or phrases that they repeated over and over. If you tried to translate these repeated phrases into sentences, you lost the reality somehow of what was being said. She wondered, had modern America changed so much that its truth refused to fit into sentence form?

Which part of speech is primal?

Of the eight parts of speech, which comes first? Up to now, we have considered language in terms of the Two with the sentence and its modifiers relating or balancing the verb and the noun. Conceptually, this means that the sentence carries the unity of our thought through the Two, action (verb) and the doer or receiver of the action (noun in its role of subject or object).

In classical and the classically derived languages, the verb is primary. If you learn the verb in Greek, you know the language, for the construction of the noun and of adjectives and adverbs are formed by inflections. In English, the primariness of verb is not so clear. We are hard put to ascribe to one of them the certainty of primal conception. We can see that a word is primal if we have to add prefixes or suffixes to its other aspects. In the following list, the verb is primal if the noun or the adjective is formed by adding *-ing*, *-ed*, *-er*, or *-en*. But in many cases, the verb and noun are the same. See the noun *handle* and the verb *handle*, or the noun *wave* and the verb *wave*. How were these concepts first thought? The word *pray* may first have been thought of as an action, since we add *-er* for the act of prayer or the person doing the praying.

The verb usually means what it is. But a noun may have three or four permutations. There is the distinction between subject and object, as in *payer* and *payee*; between *act* and *actor*, as in *shaving*, *shave*, and *shaver*; between the sexes, as in *poet* and *poetess* (though this concept has generated accusations for discrimination and in addition does not have a translatable verb); and even between the act and the immediacy of the act, as in *jump* and *jumping*.

Verb/noun as primal

Verb	Noun	Adjective
handle	handle	handled
wave	wave	wavy, waved
mistake	mistake	mistaken
pray	prayer	prayerful
practice	practice	practical, practiced
shave	shaving, shaver, shave	shaved, shaven

salt	salt	salty, salted
shape	shape	shape, shapely, shaping
comfort	comfort, comforter	comfortable, comforted, comforting
fall	fall, fallen (ones),	fallen, falling, falling, felled
fill	fill	full, filled
jump	jump, jumping, jumper	jumping
joke	joke, joker	jokey, jocular, jocund
shut	shutter (blind)	shut
square	square	square, squared
comicalize	comedy, comic	comic, comical
(a poor verb)		
beg	beggary, beggar, begging	beggared, begging, begged

The adjective

But there are certain conceptions that defy primal expression as either verbs or nouns. Color, taste, size, sensation, quality, and number can be primal. But they modify. They are adjectives. Look at the following list of adjectives. The adjective aspect is dominant. Their noun is often formed by the suffix *-ness*. And the verb is formed by adding *-en*.

How can you describe the idea *loud* through any part of speech but the adjective? Even the noun requires the ending *-ness*, making it subordinate. And there is no way of expressing *loud* directly as a verb. What would you say? *Loudify?*

None of the numbers can yield a verb. You have to go the route of using *make* or *put*. Or would you *nine* something, or *sixify* it? It is interesting that a tit-for-tat action takes place when you change an adjective to a verb. Just as we saw that the verb *fall* becomes an adjective by adding *-en*, we now see that the adjective *red* can only become a verb by adding *-en*.

And if we make an adjective become a noun by methods other than using *-ness*, by preceding the adjective with an article, for instance (*big: the big*), it elevates the idea in an unnatural way.

Adjectives as primal

Adjective	Noun	Verb
sharp	sharp(card)	sharpen
round	round, roundness	round
sour	sourness	sour
hard	the hard, hardship, hardihood	harden
soft	softy, softness	soften
short	short, shortness	shorten
big	the big, bigness	biggen
blue	blue (into the blue), blueing, blueness, the blues	blue (her hair)
dead	dead, deadness	deaden
empty, emptier	empties (bottles), emptiness,	empty
green	greening, green	green
yellow	yellow	yellow
loud	loudness	———
sweet	sweetness, sweets,	sweeten
hot	heat	heat (up)
eight	eight	———
two	two, twosome	———
nine	nine	———
red	Red (Communist)	redden

The next exercise is a practice in breaking down the differences in parts of speech to illuminate the concept of the word behind the different roles. It involves word shifts to different parts of speech.

Exercise 12: Word shift/part of speech breakdown

Write a series of sentences with a plot or progression. In the sentence there must be a key word. Change this word in its usage from:

1. a verb into a noun
2. a noun into an adjective
3. an adjective into a verb
4. a verb into an adverb
5. an adverb into a verb
6. a verb into an adjective
7. an adjective into a noun

8. and back into its key position—the same usage, perhaps the same sentence that you began with.

If you wish to change the order, do so, but include all eight changes. The order in which you do these changes does not matter. But make the piece interesting in its own right, as well as an illustration of the properties and possibilities of these four parts of speech. It should interest or delight as content, and it should make us aware of the "changes" (differences, similarities, or simply the relationships) of the essential concept of the word.

Example:

"Objective Test"

Noun: The *circle* circled her.
Adjective: They put the *circular* question.
Verb: She *circled* a circular answer.
Adverb: The *circularly* questioned answer was a circle
Verb: They clasped hands, enraged, and *circled* tighter.
Adjective: She made a *circular* attempt to escape, leaping into a somersault.
Noun: They lassoed her head, pulled it off her body, squeezed the *circle*, and turned her into a question mark.

The whole conveyed in three parts

The idea of the Three as a cosmic unit, as a whole, is indisputable in nature, science, mathematics, psychology, and religion. The Trinity of Father, Son, and

Holy Ghost comes first to mind, but every mythology seems to have its three-in-one: in Egypt, Osiris, Isis, and Horus; in Israel, Adam, Eve, the Serpent; in Greece, earth, heaven, and underworld. Philosophy describes thesis, antithesis, and metathesis or synthesis. There are beginning, middle, and end; positive, negative, and neutral; present, past, and future; animal, vegetable, and mineral.

If we move away from the classical Twoness of the sentence and consider our grammar in another way, we arrive at the Three in the form of verb, noun, and modifier (adjective or adverb).

Verbals as the third element

Quite simply, verbals are the only words we have that *share* the qualities of verb, noun, and modifier.

Definition: A *verbal* is a word derived from a verb but incapable of making a complete assertion. There are three types of verbals: (1) infinitive; (2) participle; (3) gerund. The *infinitive* acts as a noun, or an adjective, or as an adverb. The *participle* acts as an adjective. The *gerund* acts as a noun.

Verbals as continuous and kinetic

The basic property of the verbal is *motion* or *being*, which it derives from its father, the verb. When we can take the idea of motion or being from the verb and turn it into a noun by using the gerund, an adjective by using the participle, or noun, adjective, or adverb by using the infinitive, we have arrived at an idea of the whole achieved by three parts of speech, not two.

The infinitive

Definition: The first principal part of a verb, usually preceded by the word *to*, most frequently used as a noun. But it can also be used as a modifier, either an adjective or an adverb. It has a present tense (*to laugh*) and a perfect tense (*to have laughed*). As a noun, it can be used as subject or object, can complete a verb, and can be modified itself by an adverb.

Of all the verbals, the infinitive is the most abstract. Although it derives directly from the verb, the word *to*, which in itself in this context is no part of speech at all, merely part of the infinitive, may be the agent that gives us this abstract feeling.

If the major characteristic of any verbal is the idea of motion or being, the *to* sounds graceless, positively awkward, like the clonk of a wooden shoe or the sound of a nail in a coffin. It locks the motion. But then in deadening it, it levitates it. We know *to* as a preposition, but in the infinitive, though it stops the motion, it translates the essence of the verb into the abstract, giving it transcendence. The following exercise should make us feel this transcendence.

Although there are only two bona fide infinitives, there are further reaches of meaning in the idea of the infinitive. Such abstraction veers on the borderline of the ridiculous when, as in the list following, we try to achieve an active future, a passive present, perfect, and future, or the difference between a completed and a continuous future. And it requires all sorts of helping mechanisms.

	Active	Passive
Completed present:	to see	to be seen
Continuous present:	to be seeing	
Completed present perfect:	to have seen	to have been seen
Continuous present perfect:	to have been seeing	
Completed future:	to be going to see	to be going to be seen
Continuous future:	to be going to be seeing	

But, although a catalogue of infinitives may be essentially a musical idea, the practice of arranging such a list could not give more substantial reality to our sense of abstraction. What is more concrete than this description of tortures suffered by dissident students in a dictatorship than this stanza from Romanian writer Vasile Sofinet's poem, "The Attack:"

> Strangled in the chest:
> Feelings,
> With infinitive:
> to hit,
> to knock down,
> to pass,
> to survive.

Exercise 13: Infinitive exercise

Write a succession of infinitives so that it shows a progression with sense or purpose. Try not to use words other than the infinitive alone. Don't even let the infinitive have an object.

Examples, by Michael Van Hecke:

"Orchestra"

To conceive
to compose
to arrange
to conduct
to tap-tap
to pause
to toot
to boom
to boom

"The Salesman"

The Salesman	The Housewife
To knock	To ignore
To pound	To answer
To smile	To stare
To explain	To listen
To cajole	To refuse
To appeal	To reconsider
To flatter	To relent
To flirt	To buy
To confirm	To sign
To smile	To smile
To go	To shut
To rejoice	To doubt

The Narrator

Too late
To be taken.

———

The participle

Definition: The participle is derived from a verb and acts as an adjective. It is like a verb in that it may be modified by an adverb and may take an object. It is like an adjective in that it modifies a substantive and may be modified by an adverb. There are two participles: present (*laughing*) and past (*laughed*).

Present participle. The *present participle* ends in *-ing*. Because of this, it is often confused with the *gerund*, which also ends in *-ing*. The difference between them is always easy to determine, however, because the participle is an adjective, the gerund a noun. Examples:

> I heard a crow *laughing* (participle) in the woods.
> *Laughing* in the woods (gerund) is a crow's favorite activity.

Past participle. The *past participle* is so far gone into adjectivehood that you can often forget that it derives from a verb. Look at these two sentences:

> The sharp [adjective] ingredient might be either oregano or basil.
> The added [past participle] ingredient might be either oregano or basil.

The word *sharp* is a primal adjective. *Added* is derived from the verb *add*. The noun-derived adjective would be *additional*. The noun would be *addition*. And so you would be justified in considering the use of *added* above as a participle acting as an adjective. It would be clearer as a past participle, however, if the sentence read:

> The ingredient added might be either oregano or basil.

Position. The most important thing about participles, both present and past, is their geographical position in the sentence. According to strict code, a participle should be kept close to the word it modifies.

The geography of participles and participial phrases determines the fate of the sojourner into the sentence, and some of the greatest advances in American prose style as well as some of the most inglorious gaffes have been the result. If the participial phrase drifts off course, the wrecked sentence is due to a *dangling participle*. The sport of identifying hilarious examples is beloved by schoolteachers and editors and is guaranteed to make you feel superior. Here are some examples collected over the years:

> The President made some vigorous remarks about Communists rising from his desk during the press conference.

Abraham Lincoln wrote the Gettysburg Address while traveling from Washington on the back of an envelope.
The new house was built by Mrs. Borden who later became Mrs. Gruber at a cost of $200,000.
This bank approves loans to reliable individuals of any size.
This exhibition consists of nearly 90 works by American photographers executed between 1850 and 1980.
I sat next to a man who had a wooden leg named George Carpenter.

Exercise 14: Misplaced modifiers

Find three examples of misplaced modifiers in newspapers, old school notebooks, or magazines. Then write three more of your own.

The nominative absolute. Before leaving the participle, we should look at an extinct form of construction derived from Latin, a favorite of such writers as Caesar and Cicero, which is an affront to persnickety grammarians who excel at keeping their participles from dangling. This grammatical dinosaur is called the nominative absolute. Here is an example:

> The hordes having crowded into the city, the king issued an edict commanding all units to man the gates.

The phrase "hordes having crowded into the city" stands alone insofar as it does not modify "king." Yet it is distinctly participial. The phrase modifies nothing; it has an independent position and an independent authority.

The more acceptable way to write the same sentence in this day and age would be:

> When the hordes had crowded into the city, the king issued an edict commanding all units to man the gates.

The gerund. The gerund is formed by adding -*ing* to a verb. It acts as a noun, but shares the nature of the verb. As a noun, it can perform the functions of a noun, be a subject or an object, and be modified by an adjective ("Blatant lying takes gall, even for a blatant liar"). As a verb, it can take an object and be modified by an adverb ("Blatantly passing the buck is the greatest asset a bureaucrat can possess").

In the sentence "Seeing stars upon the plain makes bitterness and woe in vain," the gerund "seeing" takes an object "stars." It also has an adverbial modifier, the prepositional phrase "upon the plain," which answers the question "where?"

Continuity

Motion and being turn into a noun. It is this everlasting continuity that is the gerund's major aspect. Although it has tenses and the passive and active voice, it is seen mostly in the present tense. But it is always continuous. The *-ing* makes it so. It means the act itself or the essence itself. As such, it is always going on eternally and defies the concept of completion.

Exercise 15: Verbal wordplay

Choose a verb from which you can derive the three types of verbals (infinitive, gerund, and participle). Write a story or anecdote (it may be a paragraph, but no longer than one-and-a-half pages). Use your chosen verb in every possible verbal form. Run the gamut but remember it should be a story with a plot.

Common verbs are better because they have more meanings and possibilities. They can be varied by changing prepositions. Make use of homonyms, puns, sound-alikes, and the music of verb and verbals. Also use repetition.

Example, by John Sasser:

"Golf"

> I glanced up from putting to see if the girl in orange was there. She was good luck and I hoped she'd put in an appearance on the 18th hole. Putting my hands back on the putter, I saw her.
> The crowd put up a big shout and I took off my hat. Putting it back on, I put my finger to my lips. Stay put, I shouted.
> I put my hand in my pocket as I put the question. She put her knuckle to her mouth when I put forth my proposition.
> Put yourself in my place.
> I put her to the test. I put my arm around her. I thought she would put up an argument. But she walked to my car. When I put my clubs in back, she grabbed my putter and got in.

Putting the car in gear, we putt-putted to her place. She made me put the car out of sight.

Puttering for her keys, she put her pocketbook on her hip and pursed her lips. I put my hand on her cheek and put my foot in my mouth.

First, put out the cat, she said.

What a put-on, I thought.

Put out the light, she said.

I picked up the cat and put out the light.

My foot kicked a chair leg.

She put her blouse at the foot of the bed.

I put out the cat and closed the door.

My landlord would put me out if he knew, she said.

You're putting me in a weird position, she said.

Putting me off turned me on.

Listen, honey, I can't put up with being put down. I put my hand on her knee.

Don't put your hand on my knee.

I put up my fists to put her in her place. She'll never put out, I thought, after putting myself out coming here.

But suddenly she put her mouth against my ear, purring like a putty-cat. At last, some input. I was putty in her hands.

6. Verbals and the Idea of Continuance

Artists of the -ing

The *-ing* has always been a part of colloquial American speech. For example, Mark Twain, Ernest Hemingway, and William Faulkner emphasize the colloquial preference for continuous action over completed action.

In the following excerpt from *Huckleberry Finn*, by Mark Twain, we see *-ing* words as verbs, participles, and gerunds. The verbs appear in italics. The participles are underlined, the gerunds in bold. Twain speaks in Huck Finn's voice. The passage is a yarn, an antistandard form about a steamboat as it ploughs over the raft on which Huck is sailing the great river.

> Well, here she comes, and we said she *was going* to try and shave us but she didn't seem to be sheering off a bit. She was a big one and she *was coming* in a hurry, too, <u>looking</u> like a black cloud with rows of glow-worms around it, but all of a sudden she bulged out, big and scary, with a long row of wide-open furnace doors <u>shining</u> like red-hot teeth and her monstrous bows and guards <u>hanging</u> right over us. There was a yell at us and a **jingling** of bells to stop the engines, a powwow of **cussing**, and **whistling** of steam—and as Jim went overboard on one side and I on the other, she come <u>smashing</u> straight through the raft.

Hemingway continues the tradition of *-ing*. The first paragraph of *A Farewell to Arms* begins with a statement that contains one adjective. It continues with a sentence that has four adjectives and one present participle. The third sentence contains no single-word modifiers at all. And the fourth sentence, the longest, begins with one adjective and one adverb, and moves into high gear with a heap of participles, five in all, each one continuous except one. This last sentence has a denouement in which these *-ing* verbals give way to adjectives again, and a further denouement, intellectually unrelated with no modifiers at all. The adjectives appear in italics and the participles are underlined.

> In the *late* summer of that year we lived in a house in a village that looked across the river and the plain to the mountains. In the bed of the river there were pebbles and boulders, *dry* and *white* in the sun,

and the water was *clear* and swiftly <u>moving</u> and *blue* in the channels. Troops went by the house and down the road and the dust they raised powdered the leaves of the trees. The trunks of the trees too were *dusty* and the leaves fell early that year and we saw the troops <u>marching</u> along the road and the dust <u>rising</u> and leaves, stirred by the breeze, <u>falling</u> and the soldiers <u>marching</u> and afterward the road *bare* and *white* except for the leaves.

The stylistic feature that makes this possible is the heavy use of the conjunction *and*. It is a paralleling instrument, similar to a two-armed scale, which both equalizes and contrasts modifiers. The business of contrasting begins in the second sentence with three modifiers: the adjective "clear," the present participle "moving," and then the adjective "blue." It is important to note, though, that the weight is thrown to the adjectives. You are given two adjectives, "dry" and "white," in the first part. In the second, of the three modifiers, two are adjectives, and the sole and only present participle has its power hedged or partly obscured by its adverb "swiftly." In the third sentence, you get a rest from modifiers: there are none. The fourth sentence is an all-out bombardment of continuous present participles: "marching," "rising," "falling," and "marching" modify "troops," "dust," "leaves," and "soldiers." They act as the potent center of the sentence and as its climax. But they are immediately followed by the adjectives "bare" and "white," which modify "road" in the same geographical position (after the noun) as the participles and create a coming down, the effect of a glider landing to safety, on that actual, bare, white road. In this space-conscious, geographical sentence, these two adjectives evoke the "dry" and "white" of the second sentence and anatomize Hemingway's message: that the fate of man is limited to his bare, white courage alone.

In sum, this is a dance between the modifiers of continuation (present participles) and the modifiers of completion (adjectives). Whether this was calculated by Hemingway before he honed is irrelevant. Its effect on the reader is a subliminal awareness of the difference between elements that move and elements that do not. The sentence ends with the modifiers of completion.

The climactic paragraph of Faulkner's story "Barn Burning" is a 267-word paragraph steeped in continuous present forms of the verbs "spring," "run," "know," "pause," "cease," "stumble," "trip," "scrabble," "pant," and "sob," as well as their present participles and gerunds. It mounts to the end in a seventy-five-word burst of participial tragedy describing how the child is on the road trying to get to his father,

… knowing it was too late yet still <u>running</u> even after he heard the shot and, an instant later, two shots, <u>pausing</u> now without <u>knowing</u> he had ceased to run, crying "Pap! Pap!", <u>running</u> again before he knew he had begun to run, <u>stumbling</u>, <u>tripping</u> over something and <u>scrabbling</u> up again without <u>ceasing</u> to run, <u>looking</u> backward over his shoulder at the glare as he got up, <u>running</u> on among the invisible trees, <u>panting</u>, <u>sobbing</u>, "Father! Father!"

What Faulkner has done is to throw traditional grammar to the winds and to shove verb action into *-ing* verbals, making them carry the action exactly like verbs but with no helping verb to establish them grammatically. Faulkner uses "and" a lot too, but he gets it straight from the Bible. Faulkner's style is an amalgam of Bible echoes and quasi-literate colloquial southern "thinking," somewhat as Henry James could be described as the inventor of the first colloquial American thinking style, Mark Twain notwithstanding. Henry James literally spoke his last books to a secretary.

In any case, such was the degree of Faulkner's faith in *-ing* verbals that he let them rip at all climactic moments. He used them as suspense. In some of the McCaslin stories, he makes participles run like a football player carrying the pigskin over the goal line, backing them forward, sidewise, and reverse, in all different directions, with "not only," "but also," "not because," "nor because," and "but simply," qualifications that go on for as long as a page. Once you get used to inserting yourself into this rhythm, pulled by these participles, you get the same ecstasy as if you had crossed the goal-line yourself.

This *-ing* frenzy has landed Faulkner in much trouble from such respectable critics as Elizabeth Hardwick and Denise Levertov. Their comments have ranged from admiring—that he was mad, romantic, and melodramatic—to summary—that he was a bad writer. Yet for all his flouting of traditional grammar, he is in ways more old-fashioned than Hemingway. Both are a dangerous influence on novices, but you can't talk about American writing without them or Mark Twain. They are the bedrock. Their paragraphs define the colloquial and operate by continuity. Their *-ing* verbals may have influenced how Americans think American.

Exercise 16 : Verbals versus the sentence

In this account of a motorcycle crash, supply as indicated the participles, gerunds, verbs, and adjectives.

"The Motorcycle Crash"

The sole [gerund] of his engine, [participle] and [adjective], [participle], [participle], where he thought it was [verb], [participle], [adjective], but [participle] but a caterwaul when he turned left, [participle] the wheel, [participle] "Yeah" as he whizzed from the right lane, [participle] back sharply until a click like the zonk of a cue-ball caught his rear wheel, [participle] the handlebar out of his hand, upward as if his tire were no longer in contact with the pavement but [participle] for hell, or maybe heaven, he didn't care, and [participle] nothing but free air when freedom wasn't called for, [participle] contact was coming, and [participle], [participle], so the crash could come up from behind him, from the ground where it was [verb].

Now rewrite the story keeping all the facts and descriptions intact, but using sentences.

The philosopher of -ing

If Twain, Hemingway, and Faulkner are artists of -ing, Gertrude Stein is its philosopher. The elevation of the continuous through -ing verbals stems from the same attraction to energy as the elevation of verbs, but it also involves a distrust of completion and an emphasis on becoming over being. Form is not found yet. There is hope. Everything is in process. Only process is permanent. Only the new has value. Form, once it is found, becomes useless, dead.

Gertrude Stein touched on this when she wrote about new writing as opposed to recognized writing in *Composition as Explanation*. She said that the new was merely that which hadn't made grooves in people's minds. Only when a thing had been accepted or recognized was it said to have beauty. The truth was that beauty, the beauty ascribed to a classic, was merely that which had engraved its form upon people's minds through familiarity.

If people talk in continuous verbs, participles and gerunds—if Mark Twain captured this continuity through the voice in Huckleberry Finn—then Ernest Hemingway perfected, popularized, and made it a conscious American feature. But Stein was the major influence on Hemingway. It was she who, by examining her own writing, arrived at the rationale of continuity as value.

Stein set out in *The Making of Americans* to describe exactly and truthfully every person in the world, and also to describe exactly and truthfully every type of relationship in the world. This tall order was born of her observation of people in the hospital and informed by science, which means exact observation and description. Since people spoke in repetition, she tried to imitate that reality. Repetition means beginning and going on, and then beginning and going on again, ad infinitum. It means not stopping.

Having worked on *The Making of Americans* for three years and completed a thousand pages, Stein became aware of her own writing process and turned her mind to grammar. She distinguished grammar in concepts of space and time.

In the realm of space, Picasso was her mentor. She wanted to do in writing what Picasso did in painting. He painted shapes in different phases of action or meaning. He painted his subjects on a one-dimensional plane at different distances and different relations to each other, so that the painting achieved the kind of motion or balance that came to be termed "cubism."

Before Picasso, a painting was an image in one dimension, frozen in space and time. The viewer had to imagine what went on before or after the captured moment. Through the viewer's senses, there vibrated an enlarging sensation which had to do with the meaning, but Picasso took over these prerogatives himself, painting on a one-dimensional canvas the multiplicity of a thing in its phases of being, action, and meaning in time.

Stein speculated on the three different kinds of time involved in art: the time it takes to perceive the subject, the time it takes to make the art, and the time it takes to experience the art. She constantly assessed the relationship between the process of experiencing life, the process of writing it down, and the process of experiencing what she wrote.

But different arts differ. The direct arts are graphics, music, theater, and movies. To look at a painting takes a moment. To hear music, even a small song, takes more time. A full musical work can last hours. A play may last two to five hours, a movie twenty minutes to three hours. A book is not such direct art. To experience it takes longer than to experience a painting, play, music, or movie, and the reader has to do the work. The time it takes to write a book is even longer.

Consider some of Stein's writing.

> There must then now be a description of all repeating. I will tell all the meaning to me in repeating, the loving there is in me for repeating.

There are five gerunds in that sentence. All except "meaning" and "loving," which are nouns in their own right, are objects of prepositions. John Malcolm Brinnin called Stein a participial writer, but she is more of a gerundic one, an understandable irony in view of the fact that she hated nouns because she hated completion, and nouns were too final, too summary, lacking the vibrating present.

> Loving repeating is always in children. Loving repeating is in a way earth feeling. Some children have loving repeating for little things and storytelling, some have it as a more bottom being. Slowly this comes out in them in all their children being, in their eating, playing, crying, and laughing.

The word "loving" has two possibilities of interpretation: it could be a gerund, the subject of the verb, and "repeating" would be its object (meaning: "Children love repeating"), or it could be a participle modifying "repeating." In the second line, the word "feeling" is most likely a participle modifying "earth." With such calculated ambiguity, Stein forced a reader to stop, to go behind the words, just as she had done in listening to what people in the hospital said, just as she had to do to put down what "came out of them."

> Sometimes every one becomes a whole one to me. For many years this was just forming in me. Now sometimes it takes many years for some one to be a whole one to me. ... Always more and more I know the whole history of each one ... always and always I listen and always now each one comes to be a whole one in me.

In her ambition to express the whole, Stein closed the distance between parts of speech. "Loving" and "repeating" finally can scarcely be perceived as distinct enough to be separated from each other as parts of speech. She forces the reader to an awareness of the inseparability of concepts and changes the relations in and beyond the sentence.

> I am always trying to tell the thing that a space of time is a natural thing for an American to always have inside them as something in which they are continuously moving. Think of anything, of cowboys, of movies, of detective stories, or anybody who goes anywhere or stays at home and is an American and you will realize that it is something strictly American to conceive a space that is filled, always filled with moving.

This perception of Americans is the generic one of the restless, rootless pioneer, heading westward, buying on installment and credit cards. Planned obsolescence, rent-a-car, databanks, and deficit spending. Character in flux.

Stein believed that nouns were static because they were complete. Nouns were lies because they were not *living*, not vibrantly in flux. Sentences were wrong because they expressed a noun doing a completed action. She didn't want to go from A to Z in event time. She wanted the process of A to Z to be crammed onto one plane, which is what Picasso's painting did. She didn't want to go from A to Z as a completion, which is what the grammar of a sentence does. She wanted the process of A to Z to be crammed into one word containing the continuity of all time, which is what a gerund or participle does.

At the heart, then, of her writing are: (1) her experimentation with tenses; (2) the repetition of phrases with their elements changed slightly to make a correspondence between people's conversations, a grammar of "changes"; (3) the repetition of continuous action by the use of -*ing* as gerund, participle, and continuous verb.

> I struggled with the relations between they them and then, I began with a relation between tenses ... And this brings us to the question of grammar.

English grammar she believed to be so simple that any child of thirteen could know everything there is to learn about it. "So why make a fuss about it?" she asked. She answered her own question ruefully: "However, one does."

The relations between "they," "them," and "then" is much more than a piece of wit. It is a philosophical focus on subject and object in time. In graphic terms, it indicates the people—Americans—whom Stein set out to paint, to describe in words, only to reach her great problem: how to describe them truthfully in their essence in time. Observing her own work, she discovered that her foundation demanded continuity. In practice, she has relied heavily on gerunds and participles and continuous verbs. This meant a philosophical reassessment of Standard English grammar.

So Stein developed a theorem of the historical truth of the English language: Sentences were the true prose unit of the eighteenth century. Phrases were the unit of the nineteenth. But paragraphs are the natural unit of the twentieth century, and Americans are the ideal writers, because it is they who have this "sense of the space of time" to recognize it.

7. Word Is as Word Does

Pronouns

There is a peculiar penchant in contemporary writing for the pronoun. *A pronoun is a part of speech that stands for a noun.* Lots of writing refuses proper names. Perhaps, Kafka-like, bureaucracy has made individualism irrelevant. Generic figures of male and female run through prose and poetry as faceless as Everyman, calling us to a meaning that is symbolic and existential. Boredom with nouns may be responsible, as Stein pointed out. But such writing has a premise: if collective man outweighs the sole person, then to get on with important things and to avoid sentimentality, we'd better abjure the proper name and use the pronoun.

Prepositions

The classical definition of a preposition defines it in relation to the noun: A preposition is a word used with a noun or substantive object to form a phrase that shows the relation of that object to another word in the sentence.

The fact is that with the preposition we enter an area of ambiguity. We are warned not to end our sentences with it. That warning stems from considering the preposition in relation to nouns. We practiced the preposition in relation to verbs in the loose verb story exercise. We called English loose. But is it loose, or is it filled with possibility? Since the language has never been in conformity with the grammar we inherited from Latin and Greek, the English preposition has floated in a no-man's land between noun and verb. Modern grammarians try to be corrective. They tell us that prepositions after a verb should be considered part of the verb. Though we know exactly what they are, we are in a soup of confusion. "Loose" is the catch-all phrase. And yet there is no other language in which such a small word has such great effect upon the source of energy, and so it should be appreciated in its relationship to the verb even as we respect its classical relationship to the noun. The decision whether or not to end the sentence with it is an act of artistry.

Adverbs

Adverbs are short shrifted. Writing teachers advise omitting them. They slow up language. They obscure main action as dust obscures a runner's feet. This advice, beneficial as it may be, is predicated on the limitation of the adverb's literal definition as a word used to modify a verb, adjective, or other adverb. They normally answer *how, what,* and *where.*

But the emphasis on continuity has affected this. Gertrude Stein's experimentation with continuity and repetition is mirrored by her treatment of adverbs. Since she distorted and collapsed the differentiation between verb, gerund, and participle, elevating fluidity and flux, she forced us to consider time and space. Time and space are indicated by adverbs. Stein used adverbs in series. Not only that, she used mutually exclusive adverbs. She wrote "always," "now," and "then" together as an object lesson to demand that a reader understand the atomic nature of time as well as space.

But in the 1960s, the inarticulate generation began to speak in adverbs. It was as if Stein had been a prophet. "Like" became the classic expression. People uttered disembodied adverbs, and sometimes prepositions or *-ing* verbals, suspending them in space as the ultimate comment. They split infinitives and spoke in unending series of *ands* and *buts.* The adverb *like* was the sixties' philosophical banner.

"*Like,* maybe I'll go to class, but, to, *like,* go I'd have to, *like,* set my alarm clock and, *like,* man, get up, *like,* at a reasonable hour. *Like,* there's probably no way I'm going to, *like,* make class." Some people really talked this way.

Certainly they were rejecting a unit of grammar such as the sentence because, unable to bear the intensity or integrity of their feelings, it had come to be understood as impotent and dishonest. Many of the inarticulates were intellectuals in revolt, and the revolt shaped a change in language and was passed on down to the naive and quasi-literate. The adverb became emblematic, and it spread to conjunctions and interjections.

As with its brother modifier, the adjective, the most popular things to say about the adverb concern its position. Teachers talk more about the placement of an adverb than its function, as if its function did not have enough interest. It shares the attention showered on dangling modifiers, and indeed it is a worthy and satisfying occupation to flirt with an adverb's placement vis-à-vis the verb and the subject or object. Although most adverbs do not have the versatility of *only,* that adverb will do as an example. Imagine a girl speculating about the love of her boyfriend. There is a dry, sarcastic friend mouthing asides to us. A bit cruel to such a serious meditation, but it runs the gamut of the possible shades of meaning inherent in a very versatile adverb.

"He Said That He Loved Me"

Girl	*Friend*
He said that he loved me.	
Only he said that he loved me.	
	He was the only one that said it.
He only said that he loved me.	
	He didn't really mean it.
He said only that he loved me.	
	Nothing else?
He said that only he loved me.	
	No one else loves her.
He said that he only loved me.	
	What else did he expect?
He said that he loved only me.	
	That's a lie.
He said that he loved me only.	
	Ha ha ha.

Conjunctions

E. M. Forster makes a distinction between story and plot. In a story, this happens and then something else happens and another thing and another thing and so on. The Bible, particularly the Old Testament, is a story in which Adam begets and Cain begets, and this comes to pass and that comes to pass. In a plot, the king dies, and the queen, filled with grief, dies too. The idea of cause arises. Events in the Old Testament are successive. Cause is rarely ascribed.

The universe of conjunctions contains the same distinction as between story and plot. For if a conjunction is a word used to connect words, phrases, clauses, and sentences and to show the relationship between the expressions they connect, it is the coordinating conjunctions *and, or, nor, but,* and *yet* that describe Biblical reality, and the subordinating conjunctions *although, as, because, if, than, that,* and *while* that introduce condition and cause, the stuff of plot. Correlative conjunctions are words used in pairs to connect sentence elements of equal grammatical rank. *Both ... and, not only ... but also, either ... or, neither ... (no, not, never) nor, as ... as,* and *whether ... or.* The Bible is full of correlative conjunctions too, for parallels were favored of people who lived by sky, sea, and stars.

The King James Bible has been the pervasive literary influence of American writers because of our puritan beginnings. Twentieth-century writers—especially Southerners, because of their fundamentalist environment—erected and resurrected *ands* and *buts.* Faulkner was the master of the correlative conjunction. It is the foundation of his prose.

Interjections

In the lists of parts of speech, the interjection always comes last. It forms the path to the primitive. It is the nearest word to a call, for it is an exclamatory word or phrase used independently in a sentence. It may be a sound as inherently meaningless as *ah, oh, ha, ho,* or *wow,* or as symbolic and ritualistic as *alas, hurrah,* or *abracadabra.* It may be an object or action twisted out of its original meaning by its emotion: *zounds* (God's wounds), *damn* (verb of general curse), or *shit* (expletive of excrement). Or it may contain or accumulate onomatopoeia. It is the closest to being what it is, yet widest of any meaning. Articulate and symbolic, but not grammatical, it is an address, a groan, a grunt, a cry, a lament, a scream of joy or woe, but without syntax. Exceptions are such expressions as "Joy to the world" or "Woe unto you," where the interjection acts like an imperative verb taking an object, but even these phrases are separate unto themselves. *Well* has been favored for countless emotions since Shakespeare, and such a practitioner as Dorothy Parker improvised tentative possibilities for its meaning:

"Well!" the young man said. "Well!" she said. "Well, here we are," he said. "Here we are," she said. "Aren't we? I should say we were," he said. "Eeyop! Here we are!" "Well!" she said. "Well!" he said. "Well."

Stanislavsky gave as an exercise for his acting students the words "this evening" to repeat forty times, handing them a list of forty emotions he wished them to convey. Such repetition rendered it as separate and powerful and syntaxless as an interjection. But most interjections convey their meaning well, for they are music. Music is more abstract than literal, but no less significant.

————

Exercise 17: Conjunctive interject exercise

Write a poem or dialogue using no words except:

1. interjections

2. conjunctions

3. interrogative or demonstrative pronouns

4. conjunctive adverbs

Examples:

"Iambic Dialogue," by Michael Cumpsty

> He: Wherein if not, and if not when what now?
> Because, accordingly, and likewise hence
> When furthermore because who anyhow?
> She: Besides, what then, moreover where from since?
> He: If still those consequently such and so
> Where meanwhile subsequently nevermore
> Hence also ever after but although.
> She: But nonetheless the why of and what for?
> He: Aha! Alas, oh dear, dear me, ah well.
> For God's sake, please! Oh me! Who cares? Oh hell.

"As Always," by Will Poe
Two gossipy women, speaking coyly:

> A: OH?
> B: Yes!
> A: Who?
> B: Him.
> A: What?"

B: That.
A: When?
B: Then.
A: Where?
B: There.
A: WHY?
B: Because.
A: HOW?
B: How *not?*
A: And since?
B: Once since then until when again.
A: And before *that?*
B: Almost hardly ever, but surely not never.
A: So occasionally *sometimes?*
B: Except, not only sometimes, but also usually.
A: Then frequently?
B: Always frequently.
A: Ah, if *repeatedly* always, then always.
B: Yes, as always.

Other concepts

There are concepts and quiddities of language that stray beyond the pasture of parts of speech. They are fascinating for lore and philosophy. Traditional grammarians have tried to deal with them, composing rules, but how do you treat such ideas as double negatives, tautologies, collective nouns, and possessives? The very fact that such concepts, even when allied, cannot be contained categorically by parts of speech demands our attention, for they have accrued to language through ancient traditions and obsolete practices, and they continue to defy valorous grammarians who try to corral rules.

Double negatives

A single negative is a simple concept. A double negative may be sly one-upmanship, evasion (see stock reports, public statements, etc.), witticism, sophisticated wisecracks, aphorisms, or simple ignorance. But a triple negative is even more complex and usually testifies to the slyest or most pretentious grab for affect. The triple negative was beloved of the characters of Jane Austen, who spoke in them constantly to maintain politeness while cutting the underpinnings out from each other. They were the currency of eighteenth-century writing, a testament to the sophisticated bitchiness of conversation, an art, prowess, and exercise in which contemporary people are virtually ignorant. Yet any unlettered dialect speaker can handle the triple negative easily. It has attained a poetry of the colloquial, its scheme of thought fantastic in complexity and clarity. Take this literal quote of an African American truck driver who was unloading his truck on a winter's day: "Don't wanna have us none of that down-below-zero weather no more." It is almost too quaint. Two of the negatives apply to the verb, and the third, the "no more," is an adverb telling when. Its poetry lies in the colloquial reversal of the sentence structure with its understood "we" subject, and in the fact that the description of the weather "down below zero" is a positive expression of the nadir of minuses, negatives, zero. The effect is to make negativity ripe and palpable.

Tautology

As defined by the *Oxford English Dictionary*, tautology is a repetition of the same statement, word, or phrase, especially in the immediate context, or the repetition of the same idea or statement in different words. It is saying the same thing twice, and is considered a fault of style. Yet so accustomed are we in speech and writing that we often react with irritation rather than with any cognition of what it is that irritates. Partridge has given a complete list of tautologies that are so common we do not bat an eye. Among them are:

attach together
both alike
enclosed herein
final completion
joint cooperation
just recently
link together
mix together
mutual cooperation
past history
still continue
termed as
two halves
widow woman

Some of these tautologies are irritants. But others have the charm of bumpkinish novelty, a positive aesthetic in the era of "mechanicspeak." We must be wary, however, lest we are tempted to become patronizing.

Collective nouns

Collectives are called venereal nouns because Venus, worshipped for beauty, love, and fertility, was also known as goddess of the hunt. Archivists of language love them because they give hints of the physical life and thought patterns of long ago. In an era when birds and animals have been removed by technology from close contact with humans, many of us do not know the collective terms that obtained currency in English, such as "a troop of hares," "a shrewdness of apes," or "a shoal of fish." We do know some of them: "a brood of chickens," "a flock of birds," "a school of fish," a "covey of partridges." Gone are "a route of wolves," "a leap of leopards," "a drove of kine" (this is an archaic expression that was once a cliché), "a skulk of monkeys," "a muster of peacocks," "a gaggle of geese," and "a nod of whales" or "a nod of young seals." So profound and poetic is the aesthetic of such a collective and objective aspect of nouns that its appeal is rampant. It has inspired many words and at least one dictionary, *Collective Nouns* by Ivan Sparkes. Some wordsmiths react to collective nouns like antique dwellers in an auction barn before the auction. And with the breathlessness of theologians they have even dared to improvise collective nouns of their own, therewith venturing into the territory, if not of creative artists, of wits:

a wince of dentists
a dilation of pupils
a Buckley of Bills
a mine of egotists
a nun of your business
a lot of realtors
a knot of Windsors

And so on. But perhaps all collective nouns were the sudden inspiration of some hunter suddenly saved from the gulp of a crocodile, or some farmer cleaning up after pigs or horses.

―――――

Exercise 18: Collective noun exercise

Improvise ten collective nouns. They may indicate animals, vegetables, minerals, cartoon stereotypes, people, or anything else that is collective or corporate.

_____

Possessives

We are once more in the kingdom of subjects and objects when we deal with the syntax of possession. But whether the possessor is noun or pronoun, whether the mechanism of possession is the apostrophe-*s*, or the preposition *of*, or, in the case of the pronoun, any of the possessive forms of the pronoun, the idea of possession is unabashed and unapologetic. It cannot be separated from capitalist thinking.

_____

Exercise 19: Possessive exercise

Write a poem or a dialogue containing possessed nouns. You may arrange or compose it freely, using either a noun preceded by another noun or pronoun in the possessive case: for example, "his master's voice," "snail's pace," etc. Or you may show the possession with the preposition *of*. In effect: a list, arranged to make some kind of sense or point.

Examples:

"Norman's Cousins," by Clay Carmichael and Katie Munger

> Norman's cousins went to the zoo with William Yeat's butler and Thomas's kyd. Katherine Anne's porter drove them in Ford Mattox's Ford, but Earle Stanley's gardner had to stay home because of Laurence's stern warning. We saw Pearl's buck leaping in Robert Warren's penn, and we fed it Joyce Carol's oats out of Gertrude's stein. But Bret's harte broke and he dropped all of Elmer's rice when he saw Charles's lamb being chased by Virginia's woolf. So they took a last look at dear Stephen's crane, and hopped in the car and came home again.

"Murder at the Animals' Ball: A Possessive Case,"
by Marianne Gingher

> The hat check hound's efficient paws
> Deliver into Lobster's claws
> Two ragged gloves made out of kid,
> His paisley scarf and one pet squid.
> Aunt Tarantula's many charms
> Retreat beneath her coat-of-arms.
> The tall blue hat is Robert Rat's.
> The parachute is Bertram Bat's.
> The leopard's spots are quite his own;
> A stork retrieves her pink cell phone.
> The cobra says her boa's missing,
> And that starts all the snakes to hissing.
> Theft dismays, but murder's worse,
> And as the hound returns a purse
> Belonging to Bill Beaver's gal,
> He lets go such appalling howl
> That every beast, dumbfounded, gawks,
> Then screeches, curses, yips, and squawks,
> Bellows, flabbergasts and squeals
> (Electric shocks bolt from the eels)!
> The cat's meow leaves all bereft:
> Poor goose's down is all that's left.

Summary by analogy of parts of speech

As we have seen, no categorical system can obtain the vagaries of our thought, and parts of speech as a filing system are as limited as anything else.

And yet the academy of parts of speech, by virtue of longevity and tradition, commands a certain celebration. Parts of speech are the sentinels in an array of logic. When we recognize their limitation, we are surely as iconoclastic as Stein and can measure our progress by comparison.

So what better a way to graduate than to see parts of speech in an analogy?

Exercise 20: Parts of speech essay

Write an essay classifying each part of speech (noun, verb, adjective, adverb, conjunction, preposition, interjection, and pronoun) in whatever concrete way appeals to you. That is, create an analogy or extended metaphor for the parts of speech—for example, kitchenware, human occupations, animals, etc. Explain why you have so labeled each part, giving examples.

Examples:

"Combustion Engine," by Bruce McGuire

> A good sentence is like a well-tuned internal combustion engine. Ideas are like fuel—they are combustible, slippery, and useless until they are sucked into the cylinder. There they are compressed by piston like nouns and ignited by verb sparks. Verbs are produced in the generator and modified along the primary and secondary adverb windings and distributed to the cylinders by a cam-turned syntax that must be kept in correct timing. Prepositions are like high performance headers—they may add efficiency, but they also make for a noisy rumbling sentence. The sentence is lubricated by high-grade articles and commas that keep the sentence parts from rubbing against each other. Adjectives ring the nouns and guide them up and down the cylinder. Conjunctions carry the power from the pistons along the connecting rods and crankshaft to the thematic flywheel, which keeps the engine running smooth. Unlike an internal combustion engine, there is no cooling system in a sentence. The words must drive out hot and smoking onto the page with strong torque and compressed power

"Love Words," by Jo Martin

> You are more than a pronoun to me. You have inverted my whole sentence, made me half forget my proper noun with your wonderful style and delicate rhythms. In our preposition, I feel like no other adjective I have ever felt before. Constantly, like a religious adverb, I catch myself imagining, imagining our conjunction, what our verbs would be. My hope rises like a childish interjection—an interruption in my once simple structure—to be compound.

What an antithesis of myself I have exclaimed! My every noun seems to verb intensely, as if I were on the verge of some incredible adverb I have never seen.

There are words that can't be explained; I know. But I can't help falling into the one with no logical parallel that renders me a tender solitary subject, a fragment, a phrase incomplete without the pronoun *us*.

Perhaps it would be a sad conjunction, periodic, like counting daisy-petal wishes in endless gardens of questions. But where there is a verb, mustn't there always be a noun? Can the articles and demonstrative adjectives be honestly denied? We need creations. We need real connectives.

If I am more than a pronoun to you, make me a part of your speech. Take me into your grammar. Teach me your words. Make me complex and rich as the most abstract and ambiguous noun alive.
There is a language here, waiting to be arranged. Know that you are more than a pronoun to me.

Beyond meaning

Restricting ourselves to the parts of speech and their relationships, charting the course of the revolutions in emphasis, we have placed our faith in an ideal of logic or meaning.

But there is a music in language that seduces us beyond literal meaning. Every word has a music without relation to its definition. Each vowel, each consonant in a word is a music that suffuses, repels, or beguiles. The larger structures beat rhythms that have effect as strong as their content and may be at odds with it. In fact, there is no talking about language in terms of pure meaning, and even though we practiced each exercise as a demonstration, some, such as the verbal wordplay exercise, slipped into music to make these points. For music dominates literal meaning, and no rational definition or grammar can compete.

8. Words as They Sound, Read, Mean, and Seduce

The meaning of sound

The human voice is the most sophisticated of all the musical instruments. The manmade string, woodwind, percussion, and brass of an orchestra are imitations of the human voice as well as of sounds of nature like wind through a grass blade, the drums of thunder, the whistle of a bird, or the blast of the sea.

Does sound have meaning? We feel it does, but can't specify what. We express such meaning in vague psychological terms. Yet from the beginning of time, man has acted as if there were prevailing and whole as well as particular significance in sound.

To Indian mystics, the universal holy sound is *ohm* or *aum*. It is the replica of the roar of the universe heard in nature in the roar of the sea and such natural sounds as cloud rumblings, wind, and the sound of the seashell. But the Buddhists have organized sound into an even more diverse system of meanings. They have a religious ritual based upon the mantra, a holy combination of syllable and waver, a spoken sound that corresponds to states of mankind in correlation with the supreme aspects of creation, destruction, and perfect bliss. When each man discovers his particular mantra and learns to intone it, he has mastered the foundation for his singular mode of prayer, the pathway to his union with God. The practice of the mantra is based on the conviction of universal meaning in particular sound patterns, and such is its power that life or death, harmony or destruction, can befall a man by its utterance.

Herodotus noted that the name of God was kept secret in classical Egypt because of the fearful power exerted by its audible expression. In the ancient Semitic language of Hebrew, there was an understood recognition of the difference between the sounds of vowels and consonants, vowels carrying holy etheric meaning and consonants being earthbound. It was consonants that formed specific meanings. Vowels carried the indefinite spiritual reality floating above. The Hebrew and Arabic alphabets, therefore, are based almost totally on consonants and have a dearth of symbols for vowels. The names Jacob, David, Rachel, and Joseph would be spelled JCB, DVD, RCHL, and JSPH. Certain shorthands and computer languages have borrowed this method of distinction—ironically, not for holiness, but for expediency.

Music/speech

Music and speech are both sound. Although synthesizers have brought music nearer to speech, we must differentiate. Words have literal meaning. Music conveys emotions and ideas of a different order.

One school of thought has it that instrumental music developed later than and out of singing or voice music. In Neapolitan songs, you can hear the call of shepherds from mountain to mountain. The choruses in Greek drama were speech, but stylized, with certain pitch, accents, and falls of the voice that made the chorus's speech resemble music. The oratorios, madrigals, and chorales of medieval music employed words as well as intricate patterns of notes. Opera and operetta were a later form of singing devoted to romance and story rather than prayer, mythology, or religion. Popular singing, from crooning to Broadway tunes, from rock to folk to rap, emphasizes words and beat often at the expense of melody and harmony.

Pure instrumental music in classical music from Bach to Bartok emphasizes the pattern and form of melody and harmony. The more abstract it is—that is, the more it dissociates from visual nature, story, and other arts such as painting or literature—the more it is approved of. In fact, the idea of seeing pictures or relating certain passages with certain psychological states is considered despicable. This was not always true. We hear stories of Strauss hearing birds singing in the park and writing a waltz. And in *Remembrance of Things Past*, Proust exposits on the meaning of a certain passage of Vinteuil's music as it affected the narrator and Swann throughout their lives, how it changed from era to era, and how it differed in the degree of emotion it produced at different times. Proust did not exclude the descriptive qualities of music as it related to scenes in nature. It was part of a larger analysis.

In Eastern music an instrument winds around one or two notes, like a voice experimenting or improvising in the slightest scale of difference possible. Different scales developed in the East and the West. Twentieth-century Western efforts to break out of the classical mode of the octave led to serial music. Electronic development broke the pattern of fixed notes as we know them in piano, organ, wood, and brass instrument, leading to a sound approximating both human voice and noise. Concrete and electronic music is not formal, as in pure fixed-note music, and not literal, as in music that employs words. Certain forms of pop and folk music also make instruments mimic voice, an ironical reversal of the idea of instrumental music coming from vocal song. The Caribbean music of Jamaica and the Dominican Republic is an example of music imitating speech, the percussion instruments mimicking in beat and pitch the incessant gossip of the street. Disco instrumentals also have the high-pitched sound of weird human voices. And there are rap and hip hop compositions in which voice and rhythm dispense with melody altogether.

Pure music has been classified for use as background aid in TV and cinema. There are predigested categories listed in manuals and on recording discs so producers can fit certain music to certain pictures or actions: circus, serio-tragic, joyful, interplanetary, horror, etc. Musak is another manipulative device to beguile consumers to buy or to be calm in doctors' offices. It drains texture and style from melody and renders it harmless, similar, indistinguishable—ultimately, something you don't have to listen to.

In sum the differentiation between music and speech is hard to tab, but essentially the difference lies in the employment of words with literal meaning. In the purest instrumental music, the goal is to transcend meaning in words toward a larger effect of sound forms.

Universal phonetic symbolism

To test whether there is such a thing as a universal meaning in sound, linguists classify words into phonetic units. A branch of linguistics has developed called psycholinguistics, a field of inquiry that examines language with the aims and techniques of psychology. Psycholinguists have conducted studies to determine whether there is such a thing as universal phonetic symbolism.

Do certain vowels mean the same thing in all languages? Do certain consonants mean the same thing throughout the world? And do certain combinations of the two—syllables—have a universal meaning?

The consensus is no. Yet linguists refuse to disallow the possibility completely.

Studies have been performed that examine sounds in terms of size: large/little; distance: far/near; weight: heavy/light; shape: pointed/round; movement: fast/slow; pleasantness: pleasant/unpleasant; temperature: cool/warm. Experiments have centered on (1) sound labels for nonsense objects; (2) the meanings individual sounds suggest; (3) guessing the meanings of foreign words; and (4) the appropriateness of the sounds of words for their meanings.

Onomatopoeia seems often to be universal. Look at these words for the sound of a rooster's voice:

kou-kou-ri-kou (Greek)
cock-a-doodle-doo (English)
coquelico (French)
kikeriki (German)
kykeliky (Danish)
kokyo (Korean)
kukeliku (Swedish)
kokekokkyo (Japanese)

Or these for the sound of a dog:

gavgav (Greek)
bow-wow (English)
wangwang (Japanese)
mongmong (Korean)

But no one knows where onomatopoeia ends and universal phonetic symbolism begins.

It has been suggested that short *i*, which is formed with an almost closed mouth, close to the teeth and lips, conveys the idea of nearness or littleness, where the larger, more openmouthed sound of the broad *a* vowel conveys the idea of something large, far away, and vast.

The following table compares the sound of words meaning "here" and "there" in forty-two languages. It was compiled by Charlotte Tanz in 1971 in her search for evidence for universal phonetic symbolism. "Here" and "there" are basic to any language and there are not many synonyms for them, which contributes to their suitability in an experiment.

Language Family	Language	Here	There
Indo-European			
	English	here	there
	French	ici	la
	German	hier	da
	Greek	edo	ekei
	Latin	hic	ibi
	Polish	tu	tam
	Urdu	yahen	wahan
Semitic			
	Arabic	huna	hunaka
	Hebrew	poh/hine	sham
Finno-Ugric			
	Hungarian	it^h	ot^h
Australian			
	Djirbal	bayd-i	bayd-a
Sino-Tibetan			
	Chinese Mandarin	juh lee	nah lee
	Chinese Cantonese	li	nga
Japanese			
	Japanese	koko/soko	asoko
Maya			
	Yucatec	-a'	-o'
	Tseltal	ni d(v(	ga d(v(
Uto-Aztecan			
	Aztec	nika-n	onka-n
	Papago	'ími	'á-mi

Language-specific phonetic symbolism

But if they can't prove universal phonetic symbolism, linguists agree that related languages have like sounds. This is natural to the historical development of language as a whole. Also, in a particular language such as English, a word of recognizable character in its vowel or consonant makeup generates words similar to itself.

The historical reason for sound symbolism

All European languages are related, as they stem from Indo-European. In the following words, the short *i* sound indicates smallness.

tip	English
pin	English
piccolo	Italian
chink	English
petit	French
piccino	Italian
piddling	English
midget	English
kind	German
pilt	Danish
chico	Spanish
micro	Greek
little	English
kid	English
chit	English
quisquilioe	Latin
mica	Latin
slit	English

When one language is related to another, there is definite phonetic symbolism. The *g* in German, which may be associated with bigness as in the words *gross*, *grossartig*, and *Gott* is related to the English words *grand*, *great*, *gigantic*, *giant*, *grow*, *gain*, *gargantuan*, and *God*.

To understand the correlation between word sound and word meaning in English, we must look at its historical development.

English belongs to the Indo-European language family, which includes languages spoken by half the population of the world. Indo-European as a language no longer exists. It was spoken in a prehistoric era before alphabets or writing existed, and then, it is believed, developed and split up into the major languages of India and Europe.

The oldest form of Indo-European still surviving is Sanskrit. Greek and Latin, the classical languages are closely related to Sanskrit. Greek and Latin have been the subject of study by linguists not only because of this historical connection with Sanskrit, but because of their generative development into the modern European languages.

The Indo-European language is the mother of the main languages of the modern West, but it also includes Indian, Iranian or Persian, Armenian, Celtic, Albanian, and Balto-Slavic. Greek in the larger sense is referred to as Hellenic. Latin in its larger context is called Italic, and the Romance languages, French, Italian, Spanish, Portuguese, and Romanian are derived from it. The Germanic branch fostered the Germanic languages, the north German developing into the Scandinavian tongues, and west Germanic into German, Dutch, Flemish, and English.

The relatedness of certain sounds in related languages, such as the *g* for big in German and English, was studied carefully in the nineteenth century and observed to have fallen into certain patterns. Jacob Grimm of the Grimm's fairy tale brothers formulated Grimm's Law in 1822. It showed how the Germanic language, in separating itself from the classical phase of the Indo-European family, formed a pattern of consonant change. The *p*, *b*, *f*, and *v* are related. The *t*, *d*, *th*, and *z* are related. And the *k* (*c*), *g*, *ch*, *x*, and *h* are related. It is demonstrated in the change from classical Latin and Greek to the Germanic language of English.

Classical	Germanic
Greek, Latin *pater*	*father*
Latin *pulex*	*flea*
Latin *frango*	*break*
Greek *odont-*, Latin *dent*	*tooth, Zahn*
Latin *tenuis*	*thin*
Greek *cardia*, Latin *cord-*	*heart, Harz*
Greek *octo*, Latin *octo*	*eight, acht*
Greek *chorta*, Latin *hortus*	*garden, Garten*
Greek *gonu* Latin *genu*	*knee*
Greek *thugater*	*daughter*
Latin *fero*	*bear*

Karl Verner, a Dutchman, rationalized the irregularities in Grimm's Law in 1875. It was a matter of accentuation. If the original accent had been on a different syllable in Latin or Greek, the transitional Germanic consonant went from unvoiced to voiced.

The correlation of word sounds in English, then, is germane to its historical development.

Aggregation as a reason for sound symbolism

If similarities in sound in a specific language have evolved through historical tran-
sition, they have also been generated through one word collecting similar sound-
and-mean-alikes. Certain languages are more susceptible to language-specific
phonetic symbolism than others. English is an extremely associative language,
and writers like Dickens, Lewis Carroll, and James Joyce have reveled in its possibilities and practiced them to the hilt.

The classical linguist Otto Jespersen, who was a Dane, said that the short *u* sound
was ugly, unlikable, even disgusting, and he illustrated with a consortium of
words: "blunder, bungle, bung, clumsy, humdrum, humbug, strum, slush, slub-
ber, sloven, muck, mud, scug, juggins, numbskull, dunderhead, gull." His list
inspires one to jump on the bandwagon with one's own discoveries: *crud, yuck,
ugh, butt, bug, sludge, fudge, upchuck, fuck, lug, drugs, dung, scuzzy, mundane,* and
bludgeon.

A particularly expressive word in a single language such as English generates like-
sounding words with similar meanings. *Drizzle,* for instance, which has associations with *water, down,* and *lackadaisical,* may be allied with *drip, drop, drool,
dribble, drench, drawl, drivel, bedraggled,* and *dreck.* The *dr* sound is common to
all. Jespersen cited the *f* sound in *fool* as collecting such words around it as "fop,
foozy, fogy, and fogram (old)," to which one could add *fake, phoney, fancy-man,
fatso, falsie, fathead, Alphonse, floozy, foolery, fiddle-faddle, fiddle-dee-dee,* and
folderol. The *sn* in *snide* is associated with something underhanded, crooked,
nasal-sounding, and meretricious. It generates *sneak, sniffle, snigger, snake, snag,
sniff, snafu, snoot, snicker, snarl,* and *snoop.* The *fl* sound is often associated with
fast movement as in the words: *flutter, flap, flick, flip, flash, flit, floozie, flicker, flit-
ter, flinch,* and *fling.* The sound *t* is associated with smallness as in the words *tiny,
teeny, tip, little, teeny-bopper, teensy-weensy,* and *teeny-weeny.*

We could ascribe countless reasons to the fact that short *i* or *e* suggest smallness
and nearness, where broad *a, o,* and long *u* express remoteness, largeness, and
depth. The former are high pitched compared to the latter, and small objects
make high-pitched sounds where large ones make low sounds: for example, the
mouse squeak versus the elephant trumpet, the piccolo's treble versus the bas-
soon's bass; the squirrel's chitter versus the cow's lowing. Short *i* and *e* are made by
small mouth openings while *o* and *a* demand wide openings.

But it's not our goal to make reasons. We can take note of proofs and evidence,
but our purpose is neither scientific nor academic. It is practical.

In order to escape from our stuck, literal, meaning-trapped minds, we must abjure the appropriate and embrace the inappropriate. Not because it is "fun" but because it tears us from the religion of the literal to a truth less tractable. We will exaggerate for prowess, separate sound from meaning, and repeat. We will abstract and open up gaps in meaning through sound, for in the long-forgotten games of childhood lie the clues to real literature. In all of us remain the vestiges of play-speech jumping to perform, eager and ready. The inappropriate may evoke the reasonless laughter associated with nonsense, it may produce a tenuous meaning of another order, it may hint wisdom beyond deserving, or it may lead us to abstraction beyond the ability to name. But it is guaranteed to irritate the smooth surface and make us sensitive.

Words in all sizes, shapes, and genders

Tall Words: *Title, lattice, latitude, lily, tattle, Illinois,* and *intellect* are considered to be lean and lanky. While these words get their height partly out of *t*s and *l*s and *i*s, other words may be considered tall and skinny without a lot of ascenders and descenders. Take, for example, *Abraham, peninsula,* and *ellipsis,* all tall.

Short words: Here are some nice short-fat words: *hog, yogurt, bomb, pot, bonbon, acne, plump, sop,* and *slobber.*

Sometimes a word gets its size from what it means, but sometimes it's just how the word sounds. *Acne* is a short-fat word even though *pimple*, with which it is associated, is a puny word.

Do we agree that *title, lattice, latitude, lily, tattle, Illinois,* and *intellect* could be considered lean and lanky? It is a statement based on the graphic appearance of the letters *t, l,* and *i*. Open to argument. Professional marketers are adept at manipulating and capitalizing on a consumer's biases regarding words. The *Eldorado* was a popular car, but the *Edsel* was a flop. The tall word *Eldorado* suggests elegance; the word *Edsel,* in spite of its consonants, seems less grand, even stubby by comparison. We associate *Abraham,* the Biblical and the Civil War Abraham, with tall, brooding men, and *peninsula* with a long strip of land on a map, so their meaning affects our perception of their size.

Some people associate puny words with feminine words. Words like *tissue, slipper, cute, giggle,* and *squeamish* seem distinctly feminine when compared to more masculine sounding words like *bourbon, steak,* and *socks.* Consider the synonyms "nude" and "naked." Which is masculine and which is feminine?

Comparing *puny* and *feminine* is a beck, a nod, and a pat to women. The comparison of masculine and feminine words has a lot to do with meaning, and a bit to do with sound, the letters *s, l, z* (soft consonants) being termed feminine and the hard consonants *c, k, ck,* and *p* being considered masculine. The difference between *naked* and *nude,* is arguable, but its tradition comes from Otto Jespersen's *Growth and Structure of the English Language,* which bases the distinction between masculine and feminine as the difference between the hard and soft consonant and on the femininity of the vowel. Jespersen said that when he compared English to other languages, it seemed:

> expressly *masculine,* it is the language of a grown-up man and has very little childish or feminine about it … You have none of those indistinct or half-slurred consonants or a vowel-glide … .To bring out clearly one of these points I select at random, by way of contrast, a passage from the language of Hawaii: *I kona hiki ana aku ilaila ua hookipa ia mai la oia me ke aloha pumehana loa.* Thus it goes on, no single word ends in a consonant, and a group of two or more consonants is never found. Can anyone be in doubt that even if such a language sound pleasantly and be full of music and harmony, the total impression is childlike and effeminate?

The look of a word on a page is a matter of graphic art. Medieval monks did not separate illustration from reading. Hence you have the great illuminated manuscripts (written by hand) of holy books. Nor did William Blake make any separation; all his poems were illustrated and printed in his own hand, and he did not conceive of their completeness in any other way. Modern concrete poets concentrate on the looks of type and print conforming to the meaning of the words upon the printed page. e. e. cummings's insistence on obliterating the capital letter form is a moral commitment in graphic terms.

Look at this piece of Latin nonsense concocted by Jonathan Swift in 1730.

Mollis abuti
Has an acuti,
No lasso finis,
Molli divinis.
Omi de armis tres,
Imi na dis tres
Cantu disco ver
Meas alo ver?

Inaccurate Latin as it may be, the fifth line's "armis tres" conjures All Gaul and its division into three parts. But separate the letters in a different way, disengage syllables, and you can find a conventional wooing:

> Molly is a beauty
> Has an acute eye,
> No lass so fine is
> Molly divine is.
> Oh my dear mistress
> I'm in a distress
> Can't you discover
> Me as a lover?

So we have the two senses, seeing and hearing, involved in the meaning of language. When we sit and read silently, do we hear the sound of the print? Possibly we do, based on subtle distinctions that the eye makes in assessing not only the way words look on the page, but also our perception of associative meanings that predispose us toward the lyric and melodious or not.

Actors who enroll in commercial acting courses designed to teach the skill of the two-minute commercial are assigned a sheet of color words to practice. One studio hands out the following list with instructions (typical to that competitive field) not to disseminate it at large.

Commercial Acting Course
"Color Words"

instant	welcome	velvety	irresistible
taste-good	endless	glowing	sumptuous
astounding	lavish	bright	nicest
special	savor	wide	plump
helpful	warmth	uncomfortable	worst
delicious	beauty	snuggle	exactly
great	enjoyable	absorbent	enraged
easier	eliminate	love	ordinary
cool	dreams	better	aftertaste
relax	tender	bitter	high-strung
quality	wonder	perfect	secure
edgy	rich	scream	dare
strong	natural-looking	bounce	nervous

imagine	shiny	tantalizing	faster
enjoyment	flavor	damaged	natural
healthy	goodness	moisturize	lightness
pleasure	great-tasting	bubble	deeper
pure	chewy	pampering	brawny
creamy	squeeze	thickness	magnificent
smooth	super	terrific	effective
tough	comfortable	sexy	fine
unique	spotless	glides	favorite
sparkling	beautiful	nourishing	skinny
smart	proudly	solid	robust
simple	delicate	crisp	monumental

The adjective has arrived. The emphasis is in direct opposition to that advice Anton Chekhov gives Maxim Gorky:

> You understand it at once when I say, "The man sat on the grass"; you understand it because it is clear and makes no demands on the attention. On the other hand, it is not easily understood, and it is difficult for the mind, if I write "A tall, narrow-chested, middle-sized man, with a red beard, sat on the green grass, already trampled by pedestrians, sat silently, shyly, and timidly looked about him." That is not immediately grasped by the mind, where in good writing should be grasped at once—in a second.

But the question is: is it the sound of these words that magnetizes, or is it the meaning? Half of them are clichés: relax, enjoyment, warmth, beauty, natural-looking, great-tasting, beautiful, moisturize, sexy, aftertaste, nervous, natural, magnificent. It's incumbent on the actor to pantomime, to exaggerate and emote the meaning, not to make it new. Words on the list such as *chewy, squeeze, snuggle, bubble, pampering, crisp,* and *skinny* have more potential as sounds and need less emoting from the actor. They accomplish more on their own.

In a column called "Miss Word of 1982," the word gazer and political speech-writer William Safire compared words in a beauty pageant: "Mirror, mirror on the wall: Which is the most beautiful word of all?" Safire laid down the rules. "Meaning does not count. We look only for words that the ears of the behearer find beautiful." Top runner was *azure.* A *zh* category was formed, which included *Zsa Zsa Gabor, mirage,* and *illusion. S* and *sh* sounds were prime favorites with their feminine association, producing *sunset, russet, crystalline, celestial,* and *quin-*

tessence. Among these clichés Safire mischievously suggested *syphilis* and *ravish* for contrast of meaning.

He also included a winsome word list specializing in those half consonants—the lispy-wispy *w* which brought *whisper, twilight, wonderland, windward, dawning, waterfall, awash,* and *wherewithal. M* he allied with *humming,* which he said "moves so many language-lovers." It produced *madrigal, meander,* and *mesmerizes,* as well as the most clearly and simply beautiful *moon,* which got him into such earth-motherly sounds as *bosom, mammary, maternal, salamander, llama, lemonade, pell-mell, marmalade,* and *marshmallow.* In the *v* category, he included *gravel, suave,* and *evanescent,* and in the *f, daffodil, taffeta, effervescent,* and *dolphin.* For that other half-consonant borderline vowel, *l,* he included *lullaby, laurel, lavender, lanolin, soliloquy,* Groucho Marx's favorite, *cellar door* and Monty Python's *hollow.* In a pure rhythm (rather than sound) category, he included *bumblebee, orangutan, onomatopoeia, serendipity, pussy willow,* and *tintinnabulation.*

But what is beauty and what is ugliness in a word? If Gertrude Stein said that it is what you are used to and that the new is considered ugly because it hasn't been recognized yet, it is at least a matter for such consideration that advertising agencies, TV corporations, and their offshoot organizations are constructed upon it. It therefore behooves the individual to examine what influences him so consistently and subliminally.

Exercise 21: Beautiful and Ugly Words

1.   Write ten beautiful words.

2.   Write ten ugly words

Literal meaning versus sound meaning

Literalism is the great contemporary delusion. If you wrote beautiful words with attention to literal meaning alone, you joined the people who wrote *love, peace, joy, good, azure, sylph, velvet, harmony,* or *beautiful* for beautiful words. The same for ugly. *Yuck, vomit, crud, bureaucracy, garbage,* etc. appear regularly on ugly lists. More than eighty-five percent of the people answer in terms of meaning.

So it is necessary to pry a word from its meaning. We can do this in a number of ways, among them: spoonerisms, malapropisms, puns, pure repetition, inappropriate usage, riddles, rhymes, singing games, and jokes.

The following dialogue from *The Birthday Party* by Harold Pinter focuses upon the word *succulent*. As a word it means "juicy, tasty, fleshy." The word assemblage actually contains the sound *suck*, which derives from "ME soke, souke (n), OE sucan, c. L sugere: akin to OE sugan and G saugen," not presumably related to the Latin *succulentus*, the origin of *succulent*. The *s* and the *k* sound culminate in an *l* salivating sound, so that we get a proliferation of mouth-juicing sounds, a sipping, sucking *s*, the deep swallow-gulp of *k*, and a palatal tongue-wopsing *l* for savor.

From *The Birthday Party*, by Harold Pinter

> Meg: Was it nice?
> Stanley: What?
> Meg: The fried bread.
> Stanley: Succulent.
> Meg: You shouldn't say that word.
> Stanley: What word?
> Meg: That word you said.
> Stanley: What, succulent—?
> Meg: Don't say it!
> Stanley: What's the matter with it?
> Meg: You shouldn't say that word to a married woman.

Think of authors' names in comparison to their writings. The name Geoffrey Chaucer, for instance, might invoke a mixture of pompousness and salaciousness if we imagine a high churchman (Geoffrey) leering at a belly dancer while chewing a hunk of pork (Chaucer). A character in Marianne Gingher's novel, *Bobby Rex's Greatest Hit*, observes that Percy Bysshe Shelley's name is pronounced jeerfully by high school students who make the syllables sound "full of juice."

No practitioner of the word was more attentive to the quixotries of sound and meaning than James Joyce, and it is no accident that he was an Irish tenor. When, in an academic discussion, "stream of consciousness" was mentioned in connection with the famous Molly Bloom section at the end of *Ulysses*, Joyce said, "When I hear the word 'stream' uttered with such a revolting primness, what I think of is urine and not the contemporary novel."

Joyce deals with the exchanges of meanings for like-sounding words. He moved more and more toward puns so that *Finnegan's* Wake almost becomes a compendium of the world's detritus executed in puns. This gives infinite multiplicity and possibility to all things. A dialogue between Mutt and Jute in *Finnegan's Wake* (based on the popular mid-twentieth century comic strip "Mutt and Jeff") begins with a couple of Irishmen in a pub:

> Jute.—Yutah!
> Mutt.—Mukk's pleasured.
> Jute.—Are you jeff?
> Mutt.—Somehards.
> Jute.—But you are not a jeffmute?

As the dialogue continues, the two drinkers get drunk, stutter, weave around philosophizing, and presumably end up fighting or crying in their beer. Other phrases uttered include "One eyegonblack," and "Bisons is bisons." Among many possible associations:

> "Are you Jeff": Are you deaf?
> "Somehards": sometimes, hard-of-hearing, die-hard, hard-on
> "But you are not jeffmute": deaf-mute
> "One eygonblack": A black eye. We can presume that he has been in a barroom brawl.
> "Bisons is bisons": Boys will be boys. Or it could be like poison. Also, let begones be bygones, which is a word play on "one eye gone black."

No doubt this does not explain the dialogue. What happened, or what was the fictional object, is still not clear. But it is a matter of recognizing the clues, and the dialogue is an exercise in word sounds and puns.

Exercise 22: Word Improvisation

Choose a word. The word may have intrinsic interest because of its sound, as the Pinter dialogue illustrates. Or it may be banal but obtain its interest from incongruous usage, as in "Perpendicular" below.

Write a dialogue or short paragraph improvising on the word. Be sensitive to allusions, associations, puns, and the musical possibilities of the word. A framework, situation, or gimmick will help.

Examples:

"Perpendicular," by Creighton Irons

> Scene: The living room is dark. A man and his wife, wait huddled together facing the door. We hear some scratching behind the door, then it creaks open and their adolescent son, Tommy, starts to sneak in.
> Man: Morning, Tom.
> Tom: Aw, hell!
> Woman: Boy, we've been worried sick, wonderin' where you been all … (She flicks on the light, takes a good look at her son, and emits a tiny scream.) Oh Gawd!
> Tom: Ma, it's *not* what you think!
> Man: Then what the hell is going on, son?
> Tom: It's not, it's just … I was out coon huntin' with uh, with uh, um, er, and …
> Woman: (hysterically) He's been … he's been … he's been *per*pen!
> Tom: No, Ma! No, I swear, I—
> Man: You better not swear, boy.
> Tom: But Pa …
> Man: Have you been … perpendicular?
> Tom: No! I—
> Man: You better answer me straight. It's later'n hell n my patience is just about wore out. Now tell the truth. Have you been perpendicular?
> Tom: Look, Pa—
> Man: Tommy! (*Woman sobs again loudly*) I'm not askin' you again!
> Tom: (He pauses, looks at his mother, then down at the floor. He speaks quietly) A little. (Mother wails loudly)
> Man: Wait just a dadblame minute. Did I hear you right? Because there for a second I thought you said 'a little.' I've seen a lot in my time, but I ain't ever heard of a man perpin just a little dicular.
> Tom: *All right, Pa!* Okay, okay, so maybe I've been perpendicular all night.
> (Mother's sobs reach a new level and she collapses against her husband in grief)

Tom: Oh, come off it, Ma. Being perpendicular ain't such a big deal these days.

Mom: My son's been perpendicular! (Mother continues sobbing, inconsolable)

Man:(*Over his shoulder, as he guides his wife away*) Son, you'd better get some sleep, because you got lots to answer for as soon as that cock crows.

"Olives," by Sharlene Baker

> a) olives with pimentos
> b) Oliver Twist
> c) olive oil
> d) all of the above

"Mr. Speedy," by Billy Smith

> Mr. Speedy approaches his friend who's working at a computer. Mr. Speedy is the nagging, super-efficient, self-satisfied sort of character.
> Speedy: Our time is up. Tic-tic-tic!
> Friend: What?
> Speedy: You'll never finish at this pace. You want me to come back later?
> Friend: Excuse me? Finish …?
> Speedy: Aren't cha gunna start? Time's ticking …
> Friend: Start what?
> Speedy: Tic, tic, tic, tic, tic.
> Friend: What are you making that noise for?
> Speedy: Hurrr yup; you arrre gunna be late: late late late.
> Friend (*quickly*): How am I supposed to start if I can't understand what you're asking me to do?
> Speedy: Are you gunna … tic, tic, tic … be late?
> Friend: You are not making any sense! Speak clearly!
> Speedy: Beyou … tic,tic … late?
> Friend: What? You're not even using complete sentences anymore.
> Speedy: Belated …
> Friend: WHaaa—
> Speedy (*interrupting*): … areyou belated?…
> Friend: I don't understand!
> Speedy (*not listening*): … Areyoubelate …
> Friend: Ahhhhh!

Speedy: … Areuticlate …
Friend: You're so In—
Together: Articulate!

Excerpt from "Smarmy," by Priscilla Holbrook

B: Jean! What a great outfit! I love the color on you!
J: Really, Betty? Oh, thank you!
B: Smarmy. (She pauses, then speaks a bit louder) smarmy.
J: What?
B: You look positively … smarmy.
J: Wow! Nobody ever said I looked smarmy before, Betty. Especially somebody with your good taste and ability to accessorize so splendidly.
B: (with conviction) You not only look smarmy, Jean, I'd go so far as to say that you are smarmy!
J: (She squeals with delight) Oooh! (So excited she can't stand still) Oh, Betty! Thank you! You can't mean it! Oh, but thank you!

———

Speech versus written language

People spoke before they wrote. The alphabet has existed only an infinitesimal time compared to man, perhaps no more than three thousand years. Nothing can exceed the importance of the alphabet in the development of mankind, for it fastened permanently in space by means of marks and symbols the music man makes in time.

Speech

Speech is made of breathed-out air. The human organ of speech is so complicated, involving lungs, nose, mouth, and vocal chords, that almost no one speaks precisely alike. One person can be distinguished from another. Yet there are recognizable languages and recognizable dialects.

Think of the English language as it is spoken by New Englanders, Australians, Scots, Virginians, Italian immigrants, Mississippians, Boston Irish, BBC broadcasters, and Cockneys. The variety of pronunciation seems unlimited, yet we recognize what is being said.

There are two branches of study that examine elements of speech. *Phonetics* breaks language down into mechanics and acoustics, notating the difference in symbols without direct reference to how they are used or to their meanings. *Phonemics* or *phonology* is a study founded on the linguistic unit of the phoneme, a basic unit of sound recognizable in any language. Every letter of the alphabet, whether consonant or vowel, may be considered a phoneme. So may any syllable. As distinguished from phonetics, phonemics is vitally interested in the *meaning* of the basic unit of sound. In our goal of separating sound from meaning, of abstracting, we are more interested in phonemics than in phonetics.

Phonemes

Alphabetical writing systems are considered by phonologists to be evidence that the phoneme is a unit. One letter, in principle, represents one phoneme. In *alliteration,* the beginning phoneme is repeated in successive words, as in: "Mrs. McMullins mixed mudpies, made a mistake, melting them into muck which she mopped messily from morning to midnight." In a *spoonerism,* the initial phonemes of some words get mixed up with others as in: "Our queer old dean" for "Our dear old queen" (Victoria).

But letters differ in their pronunciation according to their position and context in a word. For instance, the sound of the *k* differs in the words *kite, kiss,* and *hike.* The long *i* of *kite* makes you form the *k* farther back in your throat than the short *i* of *kiss.* And in the word *hike,* you don't push any air out past the *k* since it's the end of the word. These smaller distinctions of the *k*-sound are called *allophones.* They are not of particular interest to phonologists because they don't change the meaning of words. If they do, then they are definitely of importance.

Chinese is an example of a language in which one phoneme, by virtue of the way it is pitched, changes meaning. The phoneme *ma,* a syllable, can mean four different things when pronounced differently. *Ma* (level tone) means "mama," "mother," or "nurse"; *ma* (rising tone) means "hemp," "sesame," or "numbness"; *ma* (falling, then rising) means "horse"; and *ma* (falling tone) means "to scold."

Vowels

Vowels and diphthongs offer the most unlimited variation of sound. We have seen how the Semitic languages, Hebrew and Arabic, are poor in vowel notation, vowels being considered cosmic in meaning, and how they make most of their distinctions in meaning through consonants. Vowels are hardest to limit in meaning. They can cause unending confusion.

The word *been* as pronounced by an American could be understood by an Englishman to refer to something containing coal or looneys. As pronounced by an Englishman, it could be understood by an American to be a lima, a string, or a pinto.

The following sentence contains all the main English vowel sounds: "Aye, who would know aught of art must learn, act and then take his ease." It starts with the *oo* pursed-lip position of an owl hoot, opens up the *o* to long and then short, then opens the mouth to a broad *a*, moving the lips afterward toward the short *u*, and then closer, afterwards stretching the lips to a short a sound, closing up to a short *e*, a long *a* and a short *i* to end in the long *e* sound of a screech owl. Phoneticists have devised symbols for all these sounds.

English is rich in diphthongs—combinations of two vowel sounds—and the following sentence illustrates some of them: "Fear the poor outside the door. Beware of power: avoid the desire." Fear, poor, out, door, and avoid contain the diphthongs.

All these sounds have appropriate symbols invented by phoneticists, but we need not concern ourselves with them here. It is important mainly to understand the vast change of meaning signified in such a change of pronunciation as the difference between *man* and *men, tune* and *tone,* and *woman* and *women.*

Consonant sounds

The sounds of consonants are classified by the position of mouth, tongue, lips, and by the manner of articulation. There are voiced and unvoiced consonants.

Manner of Articulation

Plosive. Close the vocal track, hold the air back, and then suddenly let it go.

p	unvoiced
b	voiced
t	unvoiced
d	voiced

k   unvoiced

g   voiced

Fricative. Partially close the vocal track and then let the air out so that there is a rubbing together of two vocal organs, with pressure and duration. Fricative is allied with the word friction, and the fricative consonants last as long as your breath.

f   unvoiced

v   voiced

th as in *thick*   unvoiced

th as in *then*   voiced

s   unvoiced

z   voiced

sh as in *should*   unvoiced

zh as in *vision*   voiced

Affricative. A combination of plosive and fricative in which, instead of stopping the explosion, you allow the two articulating organs to open and separate slowly.

ch as in *catch*   unvoiced

dj as in *judge*   voiced

Nasal. Stop the vocal track completely and breathe the consonant through the nose. All nasals are voiced.

m   voiced

n   voiced

ng as in *-ing* words   voiced

Lateral. Stop the air stream with the tip of the tongue against the teeth ridge, and the air sneaks out both sides.

l   voiced

There are different pronunciations of *l*, tight and loose.

Semivowels. Articulate the semivowels like vowels, but they function as consonants.

r as in *ran*	voiced (*r* is dropped sometimes in dialect, as in New England *harbor*)
w as in *woe*	voiced
wh as in *why*	unvoiced
y as in yet	voiced

Positions of articulation

Bilabial. Both lips.

p, b

Labiodental. Lower lip and upper teeth.

f, v

Dental. Tip of tongue and back part of upper teeth.

th as in *thick*

th as in *then*

Alveolar. Tip or middle of tongue and alveolar ridge.

t, d

Alveo-palatal. Tip or middle of tongue and middle forward section of hard palate.

s, sh

z, zh

Velar. Root of tongue and velum or soft palate.

k, g

Palatal. Middle of tongue and hard palate. Not common in English. The sound of *gn* in French *agneau*, or *ny* in English *canyon* or Russian *nyet*.

Glottal. The glottis and vocal folds.

The Alphabet

The primary thing to consider about the English alphabet is that it is an ABC system of notation that has separated consonants from vowels. A secondary thing to consider is that it contains the history of conquests, wars, and assimilations within its spelling, so that its pronunciations are varied and irregular.

The exercises at the end of this chapter and in chapter 9 are involved with plays on sound. We shall use the conventional rather than the phonetic alphabet to convey the sound we mean, but our emphasis will always be on sound itself.

_____

Exercise 23: Musicalizing a Speech

Purpose: To practice sound as a bridge between speech and music.

Choose a famous passage. It may be a speech, poem, prayer, or nursery rhyme, but it must be so well known as to be almost a cliché. Practice sounding it with its emphases and stress on an instrument (violin, viola, cello, trombone, or other instrument that does not have fixed notes) of your choice. If you cannot use or play any instrument, make a kazoo out of a comb and tissue paper and mouth the sounds through it. Try to avoid consonants, and stress the ups and downs, the pauses and the vowel sounds, in a melodic imitation of the speech sounds. The object of the performance will be to get others to guess the piece. The more rhythmically familiar, the more guessable. Some possibilities: "The Pledge of Allegiance," "Hickory Dickory Dock," Martin Luther King's "I Have a Dream" speech, and John Kennedy's "Ask not what your country can do for you …" speech, etc. Listen to these speeches on CD. In 1969, a trombone parody of Gen. Douglas MacArthur's famous retirement speech at West Point featuring the words "Duty, honor and country" was recorded by Stuart Demptster and Robert Erickson. It is an excellent example of how to handle imitation or parody of sentimental political speeches so that they become recognizable without words. Such lines in the speech as "The long gray line has never failed us," and the ending crescendo, "Duty, honor, country (ahem). Today marks my final roll call with you. But I want you to know that when I cross the river my last conscious thoughts will be of the corps, and the corps, and the corps. I bid you farewell." come across in all their exaggerated sentimentality by the sound of the groaning trombone alone.

Exercise 24: Noises and Speech

1. What noises have disappeared from everyday life?

2. What noises can now be heard which have never been a part of everyday life in our past?

3. What is your favorite noise?

4. What consonants or vowels describe this favorite noise best? This question involves *onomatopoeia,* the formation of words in imitation of natural sounds, such as *buzz* or *hiss.*

5. Write a poem or a paragraph no longer than five sentences which employs the sound of your chosen noise, but do not use onomatopoeia.

Examples:

1. Some noises that have disappeared from everyday life:

the rattle and clink of a horse-drawn carriage

a dinner bell

ring of a typewriter carriage and clicking of typewriter keys

2. Some noises that can now be heard that were not a part of everyday life in the past:

video games

seatbelt warning scream

pushbutton electronics of telephone

scritch of Velcro fasteners

beepers on garbage trucks

3. "The Sound of a Wren," by John Adler

A wren. When a wren in the heat, by the creek, that's when, a wren, a marsh wren, will send, in the heat, by the creek, through his beak in the heat by the creek, when a wren, a marsh wren. Then he, not by the sea, not a she, but a he in the heat by the creek through his beak will speak. And it means a lot to me when a he (not a she by the sea) in the heat by the creek will speak through his beak.

"The Sound of Chomping an Apple," by Marianne Gingher

Czechoslovakia!

9. Literary High Jinks

Alliteration, Puns, Malapropisms, Nonsense, Onomatopoeia, and Fake Language

Word breaking

Take any piece of print, read aloud, and stop in the middle of a sentence. Pretend to be a broken record. Repeat the last word or two and arrive at a limbo of no meaning, a planet in the space beyond words. Suddenly you are aware of all language as a universe. This is the beginning. It is where Gertrude Stein started with *rose*.

Methods of breaking and entering words afresh vary from alliteration and its ally, spoonerism, through malapropisms, puns, riddles, rhymes, jokes, and singing games to the more abstract realm of pure rhythm. To practice one stylistic device without another is often less effective than combining methods, applying one exercise to an entirely unrelated form. Combinations should have no rhyme or reason. Trial and error give way to error and discovery. The goal is to expand meaning through the inappropriate, so any new association is a symptom of success. Your ally is instinct.

Alliteration

Alliteration is looked down upon as a form of literary affect, despite the Churchillism "Apt Alliterations Artful Are." Samuel Johnson criticized the banner "Taxation to Tyranny" as "nothing but a jingling alliteration which he [the author] ought to have despised." Yet it abounds in English poetry from Milton to Keats. "Behemoth biggest born," said Milton in *Paradise Lost*. "The Icelandic poets are said to have carried alliteration to the highest pitch of exactness," the *Oxford English Dictionary* tells us. And the form of Saxon poetry from which English came was built on alliteration rather than on rhyme.

Properly speaking, we ought not to discuss alliteration separate from rhyme. Both can have a clobbering effect if used excessively or without skill. Alliteration works best when it is wrapped in a definite rhythm. The following well-known limerick combines the pleasures of that form, with alliteration culminating in the rhyming pun.

> There was once a Young Lady of Ryde
> Who ate a green apple and died;
> The apple fermented
> Inside the lamented
> And made cider inside her inside.

Edward Lear used alliteration in collections of nonsense and in letters. In *More Nonsense, Pictures, Rhymes, Botany, etc.*, he described

> The Visibly Vicious Vulture
> who wrote some verses to a Veal-cutlet in a
> Volume bound in Vellum.

And in a letter to Chichester Fortescue, he described the monks of Mount Athos as "These muttering, miserable, mutton-hating, man-avoiding, misogynic, morose and merriment-marring, monotoning, many-mule-making, mocking, mournful, minced fish and marmelade-masticating Monx."

Nineteenth-century writers were unabashedly fond of alliteration, Charles Dickens among them. And as word play was a sport, they were unregenerate. But if serious contemporary writers are loath to use alliteration in prose, some performance artists and comedians base some of their best work on it. Here's an excerpt from a contemporary comedy skit written by Zachary Gresham. Two baseball outfielders are having a "serious" discussion during a lull in the game. Alliteration renders all possibility for seriousness nil:

First Player: I always thought clarity and celibacy walked hand-in-hand. I heard celibacy can even make one live longer!

Second Player: It is precisely so, Cecil. Celibacy sounds silly to some, but several scientists studying celibacy say celibate souls sometimes survive centuries from simply sacrificing sex.

Tongue twisters are alliteration in which the tongue becomes literally twisted and cannot be moved around fast enough for the reciter to pronounce the words properly. In some cases, the error forces out a taboo word. But stumbling over a consonant repetition is usually considered funny in itself, the humor based on the doltish victim.

> If I fell on a felon feloniously,
> Who's the felon—the felon I fell on, or me?

If you stick a stock of liquor in your locker,
It is slick to stick a lock upon your stock,
Or some joker who is slicker's going to trick you of your liquor
If you fail to lock your liquor with a lock.

Tongue twisters must be distinguished from pure alliteration, for the latter is a mild, often whimsical, and too cute emphasis upon the emotional value of the phonetic unit, while the former is a trap set up for the speaker to fall into.

Alliteration: The curious cream-colored cat that crept into the crypt crapped and crept out again.

Tongue Twisters: The shrew shrieked at the shrewd sheik; Backpackers stack sacks and packs on the back decks.

Exercise 25: Consonant Psychology

From the following lists of consonants and consonant clusters choose three. Give your emotional associations with the consonants, then write a list of words that respond to this association. Compose an alliterative sentence, preferably a tongue twister, using your selections.

Consonants	Consonant clusters	
b	br	thr
c	bl	sk
d	cr	sm
f	cl	sn
g	dr	sp
h	fr	st
j	gr	sw
k	fl	qu
l	gl	
m	pr	
n	pl	
p	sl	
r	spl	
s	tw	
t	dw	
v	spl	
w	pr	

x	scr
y	shr
z	spr
	str
	squ
	tr

Example:

sl

Associations: soft, slippery, slithery, and silken.

Associative words: slide, slick, slip, slough, slack, sloven, slaver, sliver, slurp, sly, slight, slope, slush, slobber, slattern

Sentence: Slip through the gate, Sly Slipperikin of the Celestial; kiss me slow, slake me awake, slip your slippers beneath the slat, and let us slide slender in the night, for beneath the ice floe and silence of our sleep, the slave of slander slavering wakes, and slobbers sloven, to interrupt our slivers of delight.

Exercise 26: Tongue Twister

Write a tongue twister. Let it make sense. A recognizably rhythmic form can often help to make it more effective.

Examples:

1. By Susan Campbell

If you were Hugh, who would you pursue?
Not you, you Hugh-pursuing shrew!

2. The following example, written by Susan Campbell, is alliteration applied to Noam Chomsky's eight examples of deep structure in the permutations of a sentence (see Chapter 10).

The Boa constrictor tricked Victor.
Did the boa constrictor trick Victor?
The boa constrictor didn't trick Victor.
Didn't the boa constrictor trick Victor?
Victor was tricked by the boa constrictor.
Was Victor tricked by the boa constrictor?

Victor wasn't tricked by the boa constrictor.

Wasn't Victor tricked by the boa constrictor?

3. By Bruce McGuire

Try twenty tongue twisters
Tell trendy twangy tales
Tell of tweezers, twelves, and trains
tooths and truths and old white haired Twains.

4. "Love," by Jo Martin

Love's lore lures, lifts, lingers, leaves, lies, and links.

Puns

A pun is a homonym put to a point of wit. It too is considered unworthy and is the one device that generates active participation among literate people similar to that induced by Victorian melodrama, the hiss. To the daring the pun offers challenge, for it is easier to fall flat than to succeed. Once you resort to punning, all standards crumble, and you have to attain the philosophy: "If a thing is worth doing, it is worth doing badly."

The pun of the word *pun* is the exclamation "Upon my word!"

Why then should the pun be taken seriously as a literary form? Because of taboos. A double meaning allows one to say something forbidden while appearing to say something harmless. Immunity is guaranteed because nothing bad has really been said. The punster has no responsibility for what his audience hears. It is a case where, if the language is not the sinner, then the listener who has such thoughts in his mind is.

But the pun is most provocative when its meaning is *not* pinpoint sharp, when it is left open for a reader's mind to ponder. The work of Joyce is an example. Far from being the wit that merits the hiss, it becomes a literature of meditation.

Exercise 27: Puns

1. Write a dialogue whose method is the pun. The affect of the piece should be based on a definite conceit or gimmick.

2. Write a recipe whose method is the pun.

Examples:

1. "Shakespeare Cassio-Role," by Jami Grist

1 cup Much Ado
3 cups chopped Hamlet
2 four-serving boxes Othello
1/2 summer's day with darling buds of May intact
2 tsp Julius Caesaring dash of hot Titania
1 Tybalt extract of Rosenstern.
Moor or less to taste.

2. "Leonard and George," by Tim Keppel

George: What's that up in the sky?
Leonard: A biplane.
George: Carl Sandburg.
Leonard: Carl Sandburg?
George: Ha. You get them mixed up too.
Leonard: Get who mixed up?
George: Carl Sandburg and Charles Lindbergh.
Leonard: No, I don't.
George: You just did. Hey, what do you call those kind of word associations where you—
Leonard: I call them word associations.
George: Yeah. Hey, what's on the vagina for tonight?
Leonard: A cocktail party. I'm wearing my vest.
George: Are you the vest type?
Leonard: Yeah. A transvestite.
George: Who's the girl?
Leonard: The one who played in the parade.
George: What'd she play?
Leonard: Kazoo.
George: Gezuntheit.
Leonard: Boy, the food at the Plaza Hotel tastes like food for the gods. What do you call it?
George: Amnesia?
Leonard: I don't remember.
George: What was it they fed the Hebrews?
Leonard: Manna.

George: What's manna?
Leonard: Nothing. What's the manna with you?

4. "Sin Tax," by Sharon Brody

1: So you see it all boils down to a matter of syntax.
2: Djoo say syntax?
1: Precisely. Syntax. Proper syntax.
2: Ain't no syntax what's proper. Hit jest cain't be!
1: No syntax? That's absurd!
2: Yer crazy!
1: You, my friend, are ignorant.
2: I ain't yer friend and if you ain't crazy you must be a Republican.
1: A Republican? Because I believe in logical syntax?
2: I said Republican, bein' as who else in tarnation'd have a hankerin ta put a tax on sin!? Syntax! And have the audacity to call it logical at that! Only one way left we little folks kin have us a good time fer cheap, an you aimin ta tax that, too? Syntax … sheeoot!
1: I'm afraid we're having a problem of semantics—
2: Semantics? Yer dadblamed right yer talkin bout some antics, n dang high-handed antics at that! And you may be gettin a-skeert but you won be gettin no richer. (Some antics is right! Good night in the morning … syntax!)

Malapropisms

Next door to puns are malapropisms. A malapropism is the act or habit of misusing a word so that it appears ridiculous. The name comes from its archetypal mother, Mrs. Malaprop in Sheridan's *Rivals*, but her name is generated from Latin *male*, bad, ill, combined with *propus*, proper, propriety.

Malapropisms are in the realm of found objects rather than art. They don't focus to make fun of, as in accomplished satire. Usually they stem from ignorance, having nothing to do with language prowess.

And yet they have more potential for discovery than puns. Because puns close up a concept, they act as the last word. Malapropisms open meanings up to apparently little purpose by a confusion in sound-alikes. They can produce metaphors, as in: "I rode an alligator to the top of the Empire State Building," or "a wealthy typhoon," which comes from a Norton Mockridge collection, *Fractured English*. Or they can distort an adjective with juicy aftertaste, as a newspaper did in referring to the Duchess of Windsor as a "grievous widow." Given her reputation, this is wickedly patronizing. Malapropisms are so powerful that politicians can make use of them freely as a Florida Democratic candidate for governor did when he accused his Republican opponent's wife righteously of being a "thespian" without mentioning her penchant for acting in little theater productions. That enters the realm of punning, of course. Behind a malapropism usually lies a mistake. Behind the mistake may lie a wisdom. Behind the wisdom may lie a universe.

Exercise 28: Malapropisms

Write an essay or a dialogue in which every sentence contains a malapropism.

Example:

"Vague Carpet," by Annette Overton

What color is the carpet?
Vague.
No, I mean the rental rug.
Oh, the one from Formica. Or is it the Philistines? That's a travesty, not a rug.
A what?
You hang it over the mental. You know, like in the remedial times.
A travesty.
It's not really vague, it's more brown than vague.
Well, vague is a kind of brown, isn't it?
Don't you know what color the parapet is?
I really don't. I just walk past it enigmatically. It's kafka, I think.
Some people just don't depreciate. Like you, for insistence.
Are you calling me incompetent? I have three kids!
I'm just saying it's sad you don't notice the panting on the mental.

Nonsense

Nonsense has been literature since ancient times.

The three following poems were written by Lucilius in 50 A.D.

1. Little Hermogenes is so small
He can't reach anything down at all;
Though it's on the ground, he must let it lie—
For he's so short that it's still too high.

2. Look at Marcus and take warning:
Once he tried to win a race.
Ran all night, and in the morning
Hadn't passed the starting place.

3. Gaius was so very thin
That his children, when he died,
On a box with nothing in
Wrote: "Dear Gaius is inside."

The tautological definition of nonsense is the defiance of sense. Sense means something between logic and order. There are two elements in considering nonsense. The first is the *world of nonsense*. The second is the *words of nonsense*.

The world of nonsense

Nonsense needs a tradition an order to operate against. Contrary to the conception of nonsense as being freedom to the point of disorder, it cannot be except as it is bound by the same rules of order that it distinguishes itself from. Its rule lies in the area of gradation from the inappropriate through the incongruous to the impossible. The three poems above are concerned with mutually exclusive or impossible ideas of space, size, and time. Because numbers are the most exact indicators of order, they are basic in classical nonsense.

One, two
Buckle my shoe.
Three, four
Open the door.
Five, six,
Pick up sticks
Seven, eight,
Lay them straight.

Singing and children's games often provide the gestures to accompany the nonsense of numbers. Numbers lead to series. Many nursery rhymes involve series. The following is a riddle that is answered by a progression based first on numbers, and then on puns.

The question is:
"Why are fire engines red?"

The Answer is:

One and one are two.
Two and two are four.
Three times four is twelve.
There are twelve inches in a ruler.
Queen Mary was a ruler.
Queen Mary ruled the sea.
There are fish in the sea.
The fish have fins.
The Finns fought the Russians.
The Russians are red.
Fire engines are always rushin'
That's why fire engines are red.

"A Partridge in a Pear Tree" is a song built on a series. The following children's game operates on the scheme of a series, although the goal is to break the rhyme to terminate it.

I went downtown
To see Mrs. Brown
She gave me a nickel
To buy a pickle.
The pickle was sour,
She gave me a flower.
The flower was dead,
She gave me a thread.
The thread was thin
She gave me a pin.
The pin was sharp
She gave me a harp.
The harp began to sing …

The reciter either has to finish the rhyme with "Minnie and a Minnie and a ha ha ha" or has to initiate another rhyme, for example:

(And on this harp I played:)

I love coffee, I love tea.
How many boys are stuck on me?

Other examples of series nonsense are:

1. Aunt Eliza, she jumped with surprise:
The surprise was so quick, it played her a trick;
The trick was so rare, she jumped in a chair;
The chair was so frail, she jumped in a pail;
The pail was so wet, she jumped in a net;
The net was so small, she jumped on the ball;
The ball was so round, she jumped on the ground;
And ever since then she's been turning around.

2. Solomon Grundy,
Born on a Monday,
Christened on Tuesday,
Married on Wednesday,
Took ill on Thursday,
Worse on Friday,
Died on Saturday,
Buried on Sunday—
And that was the end of Solomon Grundy. (1842)

Aunt Eliza we see in each separate motion like a cartoon. "Solomon Grundy" is a pessimistic metaphor of life based on the series of the days of the week. *There Was a Crooked Man Who Had a Crooked Cat* is a series. So are the poems "Who Killed Cock Robin," which goes through all the motions of death and the funeral, and "Old Mother Hubbard" in which she traipses to all the places of life and death, the baker, the undertaker, the alehouse, the fruiterers, etc., to bring things to her dog, who responds inappropriately in every case.

Series can involve cause. When the idea of cause and effect is flouted, you are in the world of nonsense.

The following two poems maintain exactly the laws of cause and effect, but the incident that causes the situation of the last line is omitted. It is this omission that surprises and gives the poems their impact.

Mrs. Wixon ate a pellet
All the neighbors round could smell it.
—Mildred Spencer (1936)

There was a young lady of Riga
Who rode with a smile on a tiger:

They returned from the ride
With the lady inside,
And the smile on the face of the tiger.

In the case of the first, flatulence was the cause, in the case of the second, the fact
that the tiger ate the lady and the smile moved positions as in a cartoon.

An example of direct flouting of cause is this children's verse:

I asked my father for fifteen cents
To see the elephant jump the fence.
She jumped so high she reached the sky
And she didn't come back till the last of July.

Each line sets you up for the idea of cause effecting a new sequence. Each
sequence is either impossible or irrelevant. The ultimate effect is of total irrele-
vancy, and to adults absolute anticlimax. It makes the verse worthless. But that is
why it is a delight to the child whose environment to the age of eight is steeped in
rules, for rules are the epitome of cause and effect.

Cause is only one element of logic. It is a dynamic one. Even more basic to the
world of nonsense is static logic—scheme. Any scheme is born to be flouted as
the following poem displays.

One fine October morning
In September, last July,
The moon lay thick upon the ground,
The snow shone in the sky:
The flowers were singing gaily
And the birds were in full bloom.
I went down to the cellar
To sweep the upstairs room.

The following three poems are concerned only with static logic. They are concrete, dealing with sight, smell, hearing, and body parts, and they offend every
aspect of our knowledge of basic life. They are verse of the impossible.

1. As I was coming down the stair
I met a man who wasn't there
He wasn't there again today
I wish that man would go away.

2. As I was going out one day
My head fell off and rolled away
But when I saw that it was gone,
I picked it up and put it on.

And when I got into the street
A fellow cried: "Look at your feet!"
I looked at them and sadly said:
"I've left them both asleep in bed."

3. One fine day in the middle of the night
Two dead men got up to fight,
Two blind men to see fair play,
Two dumb men to shout "Hurray!"
And two lame men to carry them away.

Elizabeth Sewell makes the observation in her study *The Field of Nonsense* that nonsense must be concrete. It has nothing in it of the ambiguous or shifting. Every character, event, and incident must be clear. When you hear "The Queen was in the parlor/Eating bread and honey," you see the Queen and the parlor, and you taste the bread and honey. And when you read about the pig who sits by the ruined pump moaning all alone, "it would have stirred a heart of stone/To see him wring his hoofs and groan/Because he could not jump," you see the pump, the pig moaning, and the wringing of his hoofs.

Edward Lear and Lewis Carroll, both precise, fussy in their ways, neat bachelors, one a mathematician, the other a graphic artist, brought nonsense to an art. It is entirely predictable that the proliferation of technological objects and corporate and abstract systems made the art of nonsense give way to the art of absurdity. Gone are the animals and characters who inhabit nonsense, swept away by the aggregate and the abstract.

From Ionesco to Albee, from Kesey to Shepard, the Absurdists draw on real artifacts and contemporary actions rather than language to achieve their absurdity. They have only to catalogue, or to present realistically, as in Joseph Heller's *Catch-22* or Ken Kesey's *One Flew over the Cuckoo's Nest*, to achieve the reputation of being surrealist truth tellers. And yet they cannot cut themselves from language. Such writers as Tom Stoppard, Sam Shepard, Eugène Ionesco, Edward Albee, Samuel Beckett, or John Lennon finally seem suspended in a reality that is language alone, rather than the world.

To understand evolution to such a state, let us examine the tenets of classical nonsense as language, or separate words.

Nonsense words

How do you make up nonsense words?

In a flash of intuition, undoubtedly. But when you look at them afterward, you see that they contain a swarm of literary devices. And they are effective to the degree that they operate in strict syntax. For the recognizable world of nonsense, syntax is the fixed equation words fit into.

In *Through the Looking Glass* Lewis Carroll explains, through his alter ego, Humpty-Dumpty, his system of composing words. When Alice asks him about his use of the word *glory* he says, "When I use a word, it means just what I choose it to mean—neither more nor less." "The question is," Alice says, "whether you *can* make words mean so many different things." "The question is," says Humpty, "Which is to be master—that's all." He talks about the word *impenetrability*. Alice tells him he's making an awful lot out of one word. He answers that when he makes a word do a lot of work, he pays it extra. He analyzes, at her request, the first verse of Jabberwocky.

'Twas brillig, and the slithy toves
Did gyre and gimble in the wabe;
All mimsy were the borogoves,
And the mome raths outgrabe.

"'Brillig' means four o'clock in the afternoon—the time when you begin broiling things for dinner. 'Slithy' means 'lithe' and 'slimy.' You see, it's like a portmanteau—there are two meanings packed up into one word."

From Carroll the idea of the *portmanteau word* found its way into English dictionaries. The word *brunch* illustrates it, the combination of breakfast and lunch.

"Toves," Humpty-Dumpty explains, are something like badgers, something like lizards, and something like a corkscrew. Toves make their nests under sundials and live on cheese. To "gyre" is to go around like a gyroscope and to "gimble" is to make holes like a gimlet. The "wabe" is the grass plot around the sundial and goes a long way in all directions. "Mimsy" is another portmanteau word, meaning "flimsy" and "miserable," and a "borogove" is a thin shabby-looking bird with its feathers sticking out all around like a mop. A "rath" is a sort of green pig, but "mome" Humpty is not certain about and conjectures that it is short for "from home," meaning that they'd lost their way. "Outgrabe" is the past tense of "outgribe," which Humpty says means something between bellowing and whistling with a kind of sneeze in the middle.

His explanations, which lexicologists and scholars have studied carefully, are inconsistent, simplistic, premeditated, and self-conscious, but they can provide a method if a nonsense writer is not musically inspired.

For nonsense words, combine the qualities of figures of speech and literary devices operating under the rules of syntax.

Onomatopoeia

Onomatopoeia, gibberish, malapropisms, puns, images, and metaphor are the fishes to be caught in the sea of association.

Onomatopoeia is the most obvious literary device. But it is limited, as one can see from this nonsense verse of Charles Dickens, 1868.

"Cannibal Song"

Choo a choo a choo tooth
Muntch, muntch, Nycey!

Choo a choo a choo tooth,
Munch, munch. Nicey!

Gibberish

Mary Sanches and Barbara Kirshenblatt-Gimblett in their book *Children's Traditional Speech Play and Child Language* make a distinction between gibberish and nonsense. They point out that gibberish employs only phonological rules, where nonsense follows both phonological and syntactic rules. The gibberish of some old traditional games alters the sound-syllables through ages of schoolyard playing. The following chant of the "eenie meenie minie moe" variety has probably been creatively improvised from generation to generation, as in the following:

Raunchy paunchy domi blowday
Hom tom toot

Nobody bobigo boo
Out goes you!

Image and Metaphor

The following Samuel Foote paragraph follows the logic of impossibility, but it also uses nonsense words. "Panjandrum" is a mock title for a pretentious official. It smacks of "Punjab" and "Pundit," a natural environment of the British conquest of India. Samuel Foote wrote it in 1755. It has a feeling of "jam," "drum," and swarming millions, and it sports a Latin ending. It has been in the English language ever since.

> So she went into the garden to cut a cabbage-leaf to make an apple pie; and at the same time a great she-bear, coming up the street, pops its head into the shop: "What! no soap?" so he died, and she very imprudently married the Barber. And there were present the Picninnies, and the Joblillies, and the Garyalies, and the grand Panjandrum himself, with the little round button at top. And they all fell to playing the game of catch-as-catch can, till the gunpowder ran out at the heels of their boots.

This is surely political, just as Mother Goose nursery rhymes were political. Political satire often is based on metaphor. That's why purists, writers who want the clearest most lucid description, are leery of metaphor. An image accomplishes what no description can ever do. The moment you have a metaphor or metaphorical association, you have the power to ridicule and create. An image is not the thing itself; in that respect it is falsification. But it is just as concrete as the thing it stands for; in that respect it is subversive. If someone asks you: "Do you realize that the rose blossoms out of the thorn?" you swallow the concept whole before you stop to recognize the lie. This is the power of image. When Rebecca West described American Communists in *The Meaning of Treason* in terms of their chins (weak and receding), she summed up the point of her book and made Communists more despicable than any amount of railing or reason could do.

There was once a young curate of Salisbury
Whose conduct was halisbury and scalisbury.
One evening in Hampshire
He took off his pampshire,
Though his vicar had told him to walisbury.

There are four nonsense words in that limerick, but the important one is "pampshire." What is a pampshire? It is the name of something, since it is possessed by him. Ostensibly it is an article of clothing. The sound of it suggests rompers, Pampers, or diapers. In any case, it is a noun.

"Halisbury" and "scalisbury" sound like harum-scarum or helter-skelter, and also scurrilous, which is often the adjective associated with conduct. In any case, they are adjectives.

But what is "walisbury"? It sounds like *waltz*, which would be mildly perverse instructions from a vicar, but the world of nonsense commands reversal if not perversal. Or *waddle*. In any case "walisbury" is not an adjective, like "halisbury" and "scalisbury"; it is part of the infinitive, and therefore a verb. Whatever the vicar told him to do, what emerges is a scandal.

Malapropisms and Transplantable Words

Malapropisms pave the way to nonsense and exemplify the saying "Ignorance is bliss." Along with malapropisms is the principle of transplanting words from their normal context, wrong usage. In fact, the transplantable word *is* a malapropism.

Such off-focus found-words are treasures for writers who want to parody characters for their ignorance, to parody rhythms and daily habits of societies, or to simply play coy with. John Lennon experiments with malapropisms in north England dialogue as a music of class and off-beat political innuendo. Lewis Carroll provides a malapropism in the "Hunting of the Snark," describing a story of woe in an "antediluvian tone." Teachers of every stripe collect the eager, ignorant writings of their students who don't know any better and provide the world with a great deal of unintended hilarity.

Spoonerisms make nonsense. A twelve-year-old girl was recorded saying, "As I walked down to the wayrail station, I met a bark and it dogged at me. I pulled a hedge out of a stake and necked its knock out." There is only one true spoonerism in this sentence, the word "wayrail." All the other transpositions are word oppositions: "bark" with "dog," "hedge" with "stake," and "neck" with "knock." "Wayrail" deals with the components of one word, the others with word switching.

The syntax of nonsense

Note the poem "The Turnip Seller," by Samuel Johnson. It contains no nonsense words, yet the nonsense turns on the word "cries," and on the sounds of "turnip" and "cry not."

"The Turnip Seller"

If a man who turnips cries,
Cry not when his father dies,
It is proof that he would rather
Have a turnip than his father.

Translation: If a man who cries "Turnips" doesn't cry when his father dies, it is proof that he would rather have a turnip than his father.

You have an impossible piece of logic, founded on syntax and sound. In the process, the repetition of the word *turnip* almost makes the word lose its meaning to become nonsense.

How does the syntax work when you deal with nonsense words? The three prime concepts, noun, adjective, and verb, must remain exact. They are integral. Lewis Carroll's rule was that sentences containing nonsense words have to look like genuine sentences bearing reference.

What part of speech, then, is best suited to be a nonsense word? Humpty-Dumpty evaluated the three. He favored first the adjective, and then the noun. Verbs have "too much temper": "They're the proudest … Adjectives you can do anything with, but not verbs."

Nouns. The nonsense noun ought not to conjure a strong image or be too associative; otherwise it will not have the lee and sway to hold an abstraction.

To make a nonsense noun recognizable, give it an article, a possessive, or an ending denoting singularity or plurality. Plurality may be expressed with an *s*, or with an *-en*, as in *children.* You can even use the Latin category of plurality, the *-us* ending changed to *-i*, the *-on* or *-un* ending (e.g., *phenomenon*) changed to *-a*, which adds a degree of sophistication or delight. Another way to distinguish the nonsense noun is to qualify it with an adjective, or a prepositional phrase or modifying clause" "The pobble who has no toes."

Some examples of nonsense nouns, many of them proper names, the names of characters or of places, have become institutionalized in English: Bandersnatch, the Quangle-Wangle, the dong with the luminous nose, faithful Wopkins, the old persons of Ickley, West Dumpet, and Bray, the sunset isles of Boshes, the Yonghy-Bonghy-Bo, a Hoddy-Doddy, the Bay of Gurtle, the Jumblies, and the snark all come from Lear and Carroll.

Adjectives. Adjectives, of all parts of speech, lend themselves to nonsense. To identify them as adjectives, use typical adjective endings: *-y*, *-ious*, *-able*, *-ible*, *-ed*, or *-en*. See the list of adjectives formed from verbs in chapter five.

Adjectives can be more associative than nouns, according to the Carroll credo. He chose the adjective to illustrate the portmanteau word. His nonsense adjectives are associative musically, rather than homonymic (the same sound for two meanings).

Image and metaphor shine in these examples from Lear and Carroll: "O frabjous day," "Come to my arms, my beamish boy!" "those frumious jaws" (portmanteau: "furious" and "fuming"), and "frumious Bandersnatch," "Borascible," "moppsikon floppsikon bear," "tulgey," "manxome," "uffish," and "scroobious."

Verbs. Why did Lewis Carroll abjure the verb as a major nonsense bearer? Because he depended on verbs too much to risk letting his nonsense fall into the abyss of disorder without them. He needed them to express the relations of his nonsense nouns and adjectives.

Nevertheless he did not refuse them altogether. "Outgribe," with its past tense "outgrabe," he defined. He invented "chortled" (portmanteau: "chuckle" and "snort"), "galumphing" (portmanteau: "gallop" and "triumphant"), and "burble" (portmanteau: a three-way meaning—"bleat," "murmur," and "warble"). They are all in Webster's, as are "gyre" and "gimble," which Carroll also defined.

Anthony Burgess generally follows the Lewis Carroll dogma in *A Clockwork Orange*, where his nonsense words have Slavic roots. He also employs British slang, Gypsy words, puns, and sheer fabrications, and in the passage below, he has only one verb of nonsense, "peet," which comes from Russian "pit," "to drink." Most readers can understand the novel perfectly well because their knowledge of English grammar and rhythm provides them with the structure of the sentence.

> There was me, that is Alex, and my three droogs, that is Pete, Georgie, and dim, Dim being really dim, and we sat in the Korova Milkbar making up our rasoodocks what to do with the evening ... The Korova Milkbar was a milk-plus mesto, and you may, O my brothers, have forgotten what these mestos were like, things changing so skorry these days ... Well, what they sold there was milk plus

something else. They had no licence for selling liquor, but there was no law yet against prodding some of the new veshches which they used to put into the old moloki ... which would give you a nice quiet horrorshow ... with lights bursting all over your mozg. Or you could peet milk with knives in it, as we used to say, and this would sharpen you up and make you ready for a bit of dirty twenty-to-one and that was what we were peeting this evening ...

droogs: *drug*, Russian for "friend"
rassoodocks: mind
mesto: *mesto*, Russian for "place"
skorry: sorry, scary
moloko: *moloko*, Russian for milk
horrorshow: pun based on *horosho*, Russian for "good"
mozg: mug

In the passage, narrator Alex describes himself and three friends, who used to meet in a milk bar and get high on drugs they put into the milk they drank. *Drugs* is a kind of antonym antidote to the Russian word for friend, *drug*, spelled "droog" by Burgess. Once you translate the nonsense words, it is perfectly understandable, and by repetition and accumulation the novel becomes fast reading. The principle is nonsense. The sense becomes clear. The novel deals with social morals.

The art and meaning of nonsense

Elizabeth Sewell insists that nonsense has nothing to do with dreams, and that it is different from lunacy or madness. She states that Lewis Carroll's verse is weak when Alice questions her sanity, for nonsense is on the side of order:

> "For it might end, you know," said Alice to herself, "in my going out altogether, like a candle. I wonder what I should be like then?" (*Alice in Wonderland*)

> "You know very well you're not real."
> "I am real!" said Alice and began to cry. (*Through the Looking Glass*)

If nonsense threatens to go into nothingness, if we question the sanity of the characters, we have lost our guides in a land of order and lost the stability of the form.

Nonsense operates by the rules of a game, Sewell says. Its medium is language. It is only by its recognizable world and syntax that it is nonsense. Otherwise, it risks a reality that places it nearer to dream, or to the modern literary realm of absurdity.

Can nonsense accomplish anything beyond astonishment and delight? Does it have emotional content? Can it achieve the high tragedy of *King Lear*, the sadness of doomed nobility of *The Cherry Orchard*, the pessimism of Flaubert, the courage and bravery of *Little Women* or *Don Quixote*, or the nostalgic pathos of people who have experienced a glory gone with the wind?

Yes. The high tragedy of *Who Killed Cock Robin* cannot be missed in the Boris Karloff, Celeste Holme, Cyril Richard recording of *Mother Goose*, though it has a musical accompaniment. The dark side of *Mother Goose* is implicit in many of the rhymes, a desolate sigh from medieval days when the sense of mortality was acute. Something of the same futility exists in Lewis Carroll's "The Aged, Aged Man," though Carroll eschewed the idea of nonsense as having emotional content, and in "The Mad Gardener's Song," which approximates absurd fiction with its last line: "He looked again, and found it was A Bar of Mottled Soap. 'A fact so dread,' he faintly said, 'Extinguishes all hope!'"

Cruelty abounds in nonsense. The cruelty of "The Walrus and the Carpenter" is not funny. After the shock of their eating the oysters, it becomes tragic. The eaters themselves bemoan a realm based upon inevitability, where they must collaborate in killing to eat. Dark is such an order. The sad stupidity of the doomed oysters, the necessity of charm, the ease of eating, and the absence the walrus and the carpenter feel is an awful paradigm of life; it overpowers the performers.

Nonsense achieves its value, at last, in terms of its content: sense. But its force lies in the musical association of meaning, and this is in the realm of magic. Its power is similar to that which the ancients found in the name of God, Hebrews in vowel sounds, and yogis in the mantra.

It is the profound ability of nonsense to establish its reality and its universe of belief in the barren wasteland of "used-up" language. It is merely disguised as lack of sense. And it is, in fact, the best of it, the symbols of our archetypes.

Exercise 29: Nonsense Writing

Write a poem or a paragraph in which the nonsense words have distinguishable overtones and are imbedded in familiar grammatical structures. If it is prose, following a familiar anecdotal, yarn, newscast, or once-upon-a-time format will aid us in knowing on some idea level what has happened.

"Somehow it seems to fill my head with ideas," Alice says of "Jabberwocky," "only I don't know exactly what they are!" Let us have our heads filled with ideas, though we don't know exactly what they are.

Examples:

1. "Greepy Inkning," by Katy Munger

It was a dormi, greepy inkning. The thitening shooped and crandered. The omining broofs gubbered in the skight. Not a nivning safit for permans or feesties, when rosoamed from the swamis a globeden monstrupitus, slipey and squamus. It fleeped, oh so skomy, cluper and cluper to the innocucent chilabies, sleepering swently by the breem. Oh! What horripities—it snukised the chilabies and swounced on their bodabies, gnabishing and cripping with its terromible fangeeths. Oh, what an inkning, an omining and horripatle inkning, when the monstrupitus went crazek.

2. "Nonsense News," by Mario Baldessari

Angry world leaders responded to the press with creebos and dibblets. Spinarkel Mayber sent a gammaglob to the Center's heskippers in which he states that "Flabwak has strobled the ideal of international hydrospliskson, and Natskrim will not be korokriegstered by his flicksten retsyn." Flabwak denied comment on the apparent inter-national stridzeeflowin caused by his infregle.

This misplaced modifier just in: The President made some vigorous remarks about Communists rising from his desk during the press conference.

And that's the works as it errs.

3. "The Spurgol Mant," by Sam Gingher

When the gilver foon brines
And the clotch kirts belve,
Hide inside your booderealm
With roor and lolt securely hellve.

The Spurgol Mant, the Spurgol Mant,
With hundeous jlades and jlaws,
Comes weathing through the worfest
To hunt for children's slaws.

Its furthing thangs how frarpful,
Its gnushing mincher blord,
Its poozing dorgal sporner,
And droozing spickal tord.

If it finds your booderealm,
Your flafe and slauw are sleuwed,
Your glones are glurped, and varteries slurped,
Your blain and brungs are chewed!

4. "Pair of Jubals," by David Krinksy

She was the kind of starkle that would boscoe your carsten if you let her. Blue dorbles, pouty stimps, and a pair of jubals that would light the City of New York for a womper and a half. She was using her blydees on me, slimping and brissing, callyhooing her jubals all over my nice, clear brattle. As she blydee-hy-hyed, her jubals carvoodled and reebled like a plecter on a hot summer's day. I was jorted, hell, who wouldn't be? But I plastered my stizzel and thought baseball.

5. Excerpt from "Love Poem," by Charles Worth

Runder me planties, I'll borgel your moles,
Den trapsie our biggest, tar flipped dar foles
So porking these cabbets or dearthing those yurts
The trekkle is morfing, so why don't we murts?

Fake language

Gone are the days when writers used the dialect writing of Uncle Remus and Kipling. Faulkner, Carson McCullers, and Eudora Welty achieve perfect Southern dialect without apostrophes. They do it with syntax and occasional off-beat spelling. The rhythm of the sentence accomplishes the accent. In the selections by Anthony Burgess, and Harold Pinter, the sounds and rhythms of Cockney or north England drive though. This distinction is more than pronunciation; it involves stress, emphasis, and the melody of English, and it entails an entirely singular perception and thought process.

It is difficult to achieve such distinctions in print. They can be illustrated better in the realm of performance. Comedians Danny Kaye, Sid Caesar, and Charlie Chaplin were the supreme artists of fake languages. The wonder is that it can be done in print at all. Yet there is an emotional level of understanding that can come through implied sound and rhythm translated to print. The following piece in the approximate sentence order of the types of sentences exercise in unit four is written in unmistakable Cockney and mocks the terms that categorize even as it obeys.

"Types of Sentences in Cockney," by Linda Craven

Simple: Most gentlemen call me what you'd call a simple Cockney.

Compound: Now a Cockney is a mate what resides in the compounds of England which is as I do and I like it.

Complex: If you don't like it or plan to get what you call a Freudian complex from it (which lots of the likes of you do), then I suggest you not go to England but stay in those parts of the world which don't happen to be those parts from which I come from.

Standard order: Some blimeys claim the standard Cockneys is cockeyed, by the by.

Inverted order: That we are inversely cuckold they'll be saying next I suppose by reason of it sounding the same as "cockeyed" and "Cockney," which is to show you their way of reasoning.

Interruption: But if I was asked to name one single outstanding human race of people, English-speaking or no, then I would have to say, thinking on it, that Cockneys has it over most folk.

Loose: Why we can eat more potatoes, drink more ale, fall down more parallel, sleep more perpendicular, and wake up with more angles in mind that Pythagorus, God keep him.

Parallelism: If you got balance, you got a man who ain't quite drunk yet, if you get my meaning, and if you got pride, why then you've got something of need to be proud of, what do you say?

Balance: Why, there's three types of men, to my thinking: there are them what finalize by degradation, which is your peasant; them what aggrandize degradation which is your polition: and them what epitomize degradation, which is your Cockneys.

Simple: I thank you simply.

The challenge both in print and in performance of fake languages is similar to that of nonsense. First, the majority of the words must be recognizable. Second, the syntax should be recognizable. In languages with different subject/verb order, such as German and Latin where verbs may end the sentences, such syntax should be followed. Third, stress and emphasis are keys to identifying the language. And fourth, the fact that different languages have different pronunciations of consonants and vowels demands their characteristic sounds. In the familiar European languages, we can analyze certain patterns in relationship to English.

In German, *th* is *d*, *w* is *v*, *t* is *ss*, *d* is *t*, *p* is *pf*, *b* is *v*, and there are many sounds of guttural *ch*, as in hocking and spitting, many *-en* endings on verbs, and many *sh* and *die* sounds.

dank	thanks	zapfen	tap		
dass	that	zunge	tongue	tochter	daughter
dann	then	zu	to	tag	day
dunn	thin	besser	better	trinken	drink
ding	thing	kessel	kettle	machen	make
durst	thirst	essen	eat	riechen	reek
dorn	thorn	lassen	let	wock	week
fuss	foot	pfad	path	wasser	water
pflanze	plant	schlafen	sleep	ein	one
given	give				
schwan	swan	bein	bone	haben	have
schnee	snow	heim	home	lieben	love

In Swedish, the *th* sound as in *thick* becomes *t*, while the *th* sound as in *then* becomes *d*.

tjock	thick	det	that
ting	thing	dem	them
tanka	think	dar	there
tre	three	fader	father
tron	throne	broder	brother

In French, there are sounds that are rare in English: the *yon* sound as in *mignon*; the pursed lip *eu* sound as in *feu*, the *eeye* sound as in *ville*, the throat-rolled *r*, the pronunciation of an *e* sound at the ends of words. In Italian, the words are spiraled within the mouth and shot out on the tongue with lots of *ello* and *etto* and *ito* noises. In Castilian Spanish, *cs* are lisped as *th*. These are the clichés of the Latin derived languages. Reading lists of words in the Latin, Italian, Spanish, and French forms one can almost hear the pronunciation.

Latin	Italian	Spanish	French	English
dicto	detto	dicho	dit	say
facto	fatto	hecho	fait	do
lacte	latte	leche	lait	milk
nocte	notte	noche	nuit	night
octo	otto	ocho	huit	eight
capillo	capello	cabello	cheveux	hair
lepore	lepre	liebre	lievre	hare
sapere	sapere	saber	savoir	to know
bibere	bevere	beber	buvoir	to drink
habere	avere	haber	avoir	to have
pede	piede	pie	pied	foot
petra	pietra	piedra	pierre	stone
decem	dieci	diez	dix	ten
morit	muore	muere	muert	(he/she/it) dies
potet	puo	puede	peu	(he/she/it) can
foco	fuoco	fuego	feu	fire

Typical Russian sounds that do not exist in English are the loose *l*, the sticking of a *ye* sound after a consonant, as in *nyet, tyelyefon, tyelyegrama*, ("no," "telephone," "telegram"), and the consonants *scha* and *shcha*, as in *Kruschev*. Although Anthony Burgess mixes Russian rather than bases *A Clockwork Orange*'s prose on it, the book retains the rhythm of lower-class England. But he has too many words in Russian to ignore.

> I could riddy a nice *malenky* statue that shone in the light of the room, so I crasted this for my own self, it like of a young thin *devotchka* standing on one noga with her rookers out, and I could see this was made of silver.

To concoct a fake language, one needs to listen to tapes and records of that speech, to listen for a concerted amount of time, and to note on paper the characteristic sounds. Farsi, the language of Iran, is an Indo-European language and is familiarly inflected, but is sung, with a hee-haw sound at the end of sentences. It also employs gutteral *ch* sounds as in German, but accented ends of words as in French. Arabic sounds like breathing into a bottle with hiccups of stops and lots of *hal a lal a bab* sounds.

For the following exercise it is more important to listen carefully than to know anything about a language. It is also important that there be enough English or English association to enable hearer or reader to get the drift.

Exercise 30: Fake Language

Purpose: Improvisation on sound and rhythm of a foreign language.

Preparation: Read aloud from Anthony Burgess's *A Clockwork Orange*. Listen to a recording of a foreign language that you do not know well or at all. Suggested languages: French, Spanish, Arabic, Greek, Persian, Swedish, Italian, or Chinese. Listen at least a half an hour nonstop and write down repetitive sounds and phrases and characteristic speech patterns.

Writing: Write a dialogue with two, three, or more characters who speak in your chosen fake language. The dialogue should not cover more than one page.

Make something happen in the skit. It should have a goal. We ought to be able to guess the language. And we should be able to understand the situation or plot. We must be able to guess what it is about, literally and emotionally.

Combine the fake foreign words with real English ones. Make the sentence construction follow that language's syntax. The combination of fake words and real words, and the repetition of words, will lend credibility. This is writing in an improvisational fake language style.

Examples:

1. "Directions for Setting a Mousetrap" (German), by Katy Munger

Sleestack un cheese tappan ze zolangahoften.

Den grapps ze zolangahoften in ze shnapps en douick till shnapps shnell unda presplate. Acht neicht, careship Zolangahoften unda shleepstack en douick ein grappers ehu les snapsto Zolangahoften vel stingabout yourn grappers. Ach neight, hunger cass un moushmush on shvincter unda shleepstack fi Zolangahoften sucflesheil.

2. "Gang Shar" or "Group Shower" (Yiddish), by Nathan Cherry

B: Ze oder dai, dees man bechan toh tak toh m e en de gang shar.
N: Een de shar? E sai "Shalom?"
B: Khen, en de shar. Bet net chashali. Deri persunol. Abit keedz et kibbutz.

N: Baruch adonai, lo!
B: Khen, et al I chuld think abit vus iss fete et de fingis e ca'rees.
N: You lo vayr shar chews? You lolayk oder men schee you nechid?
B: I dochon't. I chan't tachit aneemor.
N: Sovut you tink I kendo?
B: Cha'im schard. Chelmea!
N: Jes'dohn dripde sop, khen? Chachacha!
B: Ches net fani. Ches net chelping.
N: Ay, loochat de time!
B: Adonai, es time formi jeemclass chalredi.
N: Vel, guluck. And shalom ende shar.

3. "Noxcema Commercial" (German), by Sharon Brody

Hilda: Vas iss das, Gretchen? Vy so glum?
Gretchen: Einkeh, Hilda, Ich needen zee helpen. Mein kampf ess aufful!
H: Striekin out mit der menfolk agin?
G: Und hau! No happen nuttin. Der bachelors nein eeffen fleurten. Vy, Hilda, vy?
H: Ach, Gretchen, Es zee dreiskin.
G: Dreiskin, Hilda?
H: Ja, der dreiskin … flakin, oggly chaapin—disgustin. Zee needen Noxcema.
G: Noxcema?
H: Noxcema helpen! Ich bin ein Noxcema chik und ich bin haben deitz und deitz und deitz.
G: Noxcema machen zee dreiskin jung skin?!? Shmut skin!
H: Noxcema koen woerken wonders.
G: Noxcema, ja? Ich kandt bin worsoff for givin und trei!
Announcer: Noxcema. Fixin der dreiskin und machen zee looken jung … *Und* gettin der bachelors lookin agin.

10. Back to the Sentence Primeval

The sentence as music

There is no word, no prose, no poetry that is not music. "Run, Puff, run. See Puff run" twangs its phonic rhythm between brain and heart, even though its composers wrote it to teach children to read mechanically.

In *Fantasia of the Unconscious*, D. H. Lawrence wrote about the nonsensical singsong commands a mother gives when coaxing her little child to walk. She was not trying to scientifically explain equilibrium.

> She crouches before the child, at a little distance, and spreads her hands, "Come baby—come to mother. Come! Baby, walk! Yes, walk! Come along. A little walk to its mother. Come! Come then! Why, yes, what a pretty baby...

> Now who will tell me that this talk has any rhyme or reason? Not a spark of reason. Yet a real rhyme, or rhythm, much more important. The song and the urge of the mother's voice plays directly on the affective centers of the child, a wonderful stimulus and intuition. The words hardly matter.

Music has its revenge on reference, semantics, meaning, or information. U.S. Department of Agriculture manuals, dentistry textbooks, syntax illustrations, museum catalogues, horse-racing sheets, computer instructions, shopping advertisements, stock-market quotations, and merchandising information can be set to music. But in denotation, connotation, syllabic rhythm, syntax, and vowel and consonant sounds, they *are* music.

The sentence, as noted in chapter 4, has a structure in Twoness that is founded on its syntax or meaning. The musical structure parallels this Twoness exactly. In an ordinary sentence, the subject is named, the verb acts, and the content is observable as if set off upon a proscenium stage. The period will act to finish off and complete the thought, just as in music the tonic major three-chord (*do-mi-sol-do*) will complete the musical phrase. This tonic in conventional classical music, which is based on the octave (e.g., the work of Bach, Mozart, and Beethoven), must follow the tension of the dominant-seventh chord (*sol-ti-re-fa*). The phrases and clauses of a sentence, which are miniature forms of the Two, find their correspondence in music in the internal motifs of a main melodic structure that qualify or amplify it.

The types of sentences listed in unit four each have their music. The order as it appears in exercise eleven indicates a musical build that begins with the simple sentence, complicates with the compound and complex, varies with the standard, inverted and interrupted, assumes breadth, depth, and complexity with the loose and periodic, rises on the parallel and balanced elements, and climaxes with antithesis and gradation. This order guarantees stylistic satisfaction for the content and makes the sentences work musically.

To comprehend the relationship of a sentence to music, let us observe a standard classical piece that has accompanying words. It is best to choose a work in which the music is primary, the words secondary.

Music set with words

"Jesu Joy of Man's Desiring," music by Johann Sebastian Bach

From cantata 147. Words translated from the German version written by Martin Janus

> Jesus makes my soul to flourish, be I ill or sorrowing.
> That He may my spirit nourish, let me firmly to Him cling.
> I have Jesus; He is with me:
> He is mine though high above me.
> So I shall not from Him part, though rude sorrow break my heart.

The sentences in "Jesu Joy of Man's Desiring" are of different types:

1. Main musical line.

> Jesus makes my soul to flourish, be I ill or sorrowing.

Complex sentence. Standard order. Main clause: "Jesus makes my soul to flourish." Dependent clause: "be I ill or sorrowing." Translation: "even if I am ill or sorrowing."

2. Repeat main musical line.

> That He may my spirit nourish, let me firmly to Him cling.

Complex sentence. Inverted order. Main clause: "Let me firmly to Him cling." Dependent clause: "That He may my spirit nourish." Translation: "So that He may nourish my spirit."

3. Secondary musical line. Musical qualifier. Bridge.

I have Jesus; He is with me; He is mine though high above me.

Three amplified thoughts qualify the singer's relationship to Jesus. The stops may be considered periods, or full stops. Or they may be semicolons. If the former, they constitute three sentences. If the latter, one sentence with three parallel elements: two simple independent clauses followed by a complex, independent clause. The emotional flavor is courage in the face of fear, a clinging to the life raft of Jesus, a whistling in the dark, an invocation of Jesus as a light and a presence in the dangerous journey through dark forests of the night. The music follows the same melodic line as the beginning, but modulated into the dominant seventh.

4. Repeat main musical line.

So I shall not from Him part, though rude sorrow break my heart.

Complex sentence. Standard order. Main clause: "So I shall not from Him part." Translation: "So I shall not part from Him." Dependent clause: "though rude sorrow break my heart."

The music that dominates these words is founded melodically on the tonic major three, a chord which, when returned to, completes. The first sentence accompanies a melody in three-quarter time of eight bars. The second sentence is an exact replication.

It is the third section, with its three-tiered sentence of balance and graded complexity, which gives this work its force. It replicates the melody but in the dominant-seventh mode. The dominant seventh is always incomplete. Therefore, although its complication is a foray into new territory, it must lead back to the major tonic chord of the first and second sections. It does, and that constitutes its function as bridge. But, of course, it does more than a bridge could do. It thickens the plot. It takes a different course, a fork in the road, an exploration, a risk where the singer may get lost as the woods grow thicker and night falls. But, as melodically it contains the same formation of notes as the first and second sections, so in content the vision of Jesus is clung to as ghost, light, presence, and thus it turns out to lead back to where we started, the recognizable home, the three-chord tonic. "So I shall not from him part, though rude sorrow break my heart" repeats the original melody, completing the emotion, albeit in a subdued, anticlimactic sentence.

The Standard English sentence and classical song and chorale replicate and mirror each other. Perhaps they could never have been conceived without the song. Songs from such classical modes as "Drink to Me Only with Thine Eyes," based on the Ben Jonson poem, to such popular models as "You Are My Sunshine" illustrate the structure of sentences set in a pattern often following the A-A-B-A form of "Jesu Joy of Man's Desiring." Examples are: Scotch songs such as "Annie Laurie" and "Coming through the Rye"; Irish songs from "Danny Boy" to "'Twas the Last Rose of Summer"; Italian songs like "Santa Lucia" and "O Sole Mio"; Negro spirituals such as "Old Man River" and "Joshua Fit the Battle of Jericho"; period songs such as "Carry Me Back to Old Virginnie," "Swannee River," "Old Black Joe"; rounds such as "Frère Jacques" and "Row, Row, Row Your Boat"; popular favorites like "Home, Home on the Range" and "She'll Be Coming 'Round the Mountain When She Comes"; Christmas songs including "Silent Night," "The First Noel," and "We Three Kings of Orient Are," etc. Such familiar songs form the thought patterns that ally the sentence as structure and the A-A-B-A poem structure to the music that personifies them in our minds. It is impossible to separate the two. The music and sentences are so entirely appropriate as to form a basic vocabulary that transcends either music or language, indeed an environment, one that we accept so naturally that we are unaware of it.

But music always overpowers words. Certainly, with but few exceptions, such as Ben Jonson's "Drink to Me Only with Thine Eyes," the words are inferior. The words to "Jesu Joy of Man's Desiring" are by themselves archaic and sappy, and we can hum the chorale with full emotional complement without remembering the sentences at all.

It is when music becomes instrumental and sentences leave the beat and structure of poetry and rhyme that the difficulty of analogy between language and music becomes apparent. The equation between a sentence and a musical structure defies such obvious translation.

The following exercise is a practice in the next best thing to setting a sentence to music, or to such music, or to such melodic ups and downs and pure rhythm, as is illustrated in exercise twenty-three, "Musicalizing a Speech." It involves a replication of syllable and rhythm.

Exercise 31: Syllable-izing a Sentence

Purpose: To understand how rhythms of written sentences are exclusive of but contribute to their meanings.

1. Write down a sentence from a well-known stylist. The sentence should be a distinctive one with recognizable emphases or peculiar constructions, perhaps with inversions, or unusual placement of certain words, modifiers, or modifying phrases. Some suggestions: Winston Churchill's speeches, Nabokov, Faulkner, Grimms' Fairy Tales, Tennessee Williams, The Bible, Clifford Odets play dialogue, Dickens: a description, as of Mr. Macawber, or the conversational motif of a certain character, such as "Barkis is willing."

2. Parse the sentence.

3. Accent the sentence.

4. Write another sentence with the exact accenting and vowel sounds, made up either of nonexistent words, or a combination of nonexistent and existent. Do not use the words of the original. It will be a nonsense sentence with precise replication of rhyme.

Examples:

1. "We have nothing to fear but fear itself." (Franklin Roosevelt)
2. We: pronoun, subject of verb "have"; have: verb; nothing: object of verb "have"; to fear: infinitive phrase, adverbial, modifies "nothing"; but fear itself: adverbial phrase, modifies "nothing"
3. We have *noth*ing to *fear* but *fear* itself.
4. Knee love butting two three two three mitts elf.

1. From T. S. Eliot's "The Love Song of J. Alfred Prufrock": "In the room the women come and go/Talking of Michaelangelo"
2. In (preposition) the (article) room (object of the preposition) [prepositional phrase] the (article) women (subject) come (verb) and (conjunction) go (verb) talking (participle) of (preposition) Michaelangelo (object)
3. In the room the women come and go/Talking of Michaelangelo
4. In the boon the wee-wam hum un ho/walking on Biped out she go.

Types of sentences

The three types of sentences, **declarative**, **interrogative**, and **imperative**, embody their own music. In examining the setting of words to music in "Jesu Joy of Man's Desiring," or the setting of words to music, we have heard the music of the declarative sentence.

The interrogative sentence has a different and specific music. Its question commands a rise at the end. It is inconclusive, and its music hangs suspended. It demands conclusion somewhat in the manner of the dominant seventh. The song "Who is Sylvia?" is an example. Who is Sylvia? What is she?

The imperative sentence may be the type most directly allied with music, for there is no stated subject to keep its content away from us. It cannot be seen as upon a proscenium stage, for it collapses the distance between doer and action. The audience is the doer.

The vocative

The vocative noun refers to the person to whom a call is addressed. Antony says: "O Egypt!" referring to Cleopatra in Shakespeare's *Antony and Cleopatra*. "Maid of Athens," Byron cries in his poem about Greece. "Sing O Muse, of the wrath of Achilles," begins the *Iliad*. The vocative case accompanies a request, a call, an address, an injunction, a declaration, or a dictum. The sentence is imperative. The imperative is the most direct mode of speech, and therefore the imperative sentence is closest to poetry.

> The shepherd calls across the mountain.

The Doxology, a historical voice of the collective belief calls mankind to celebrate:

> Praise God from Whom all blessings flow;
> Praise Him, all creatures here below;
> Praise Him above, ye heavenly Host;
> Praise Father, Son and Holy Ghost.

Even the Dick and Jane readers result in an effect never intended in the goal of teaching reading through mechanical drill.

> Run, Puff, run.
> (Point of view: reader talking to Puff.)

See Puff run.
(Point of view: reader talking to child about Puff.)

They are exhortations.

Far stronger than declarative sentences, the imperative has no subject to impede its message to him who reads or hears it. It is the world of melody and rhythm rather than harmony. Nothing separates us from the action. The verb rules, exhorts, or begs. The action is for us alone. The subject, the understood "you," is us, submerged into the content. Pure music. It even leads us to interjections to complete the circle from meaning to music and back that we noted in the discussion on interjections in unit seven. Some of the interjections are verbs or nouns pulled into vocative service. *Lo! Hark! Yea! Listen! Glory! Woe! Sing!* It is no distance to breaking out of language into incantation. *Lord, have mercy! Woe is me! Glory, be!*

Analogy of grammar and music

So far we have been talking about syllable sounds and rhythm. But Leonard Bernstein attempted a more ambitious analogy, that between grammar and music, in his Norton Lecture series, entitled "The Unanswered Question," given at Harvard College in 1973.

He avoided any such vulgarity as setting words to music. He transcended the idea of equating a musical line with a parsed English sentence in Latin historical tradition. His observations are based on Noam Chomsky's ideas of transformational grammar.

Chomsky favored the idea of a universal grammar, as we have noted in unit four, because he observed that children spoke directly in sentences rather than going step by step from words. Therefore, he took the simplest sentence, "Jack loves Jill," and broke it down into its largest possible number of concepts (**permutations**). He isolated as many arrangements of thought that a simple sentence might be capable of. These he called *structure*.

1. Jack loves Jill. (Affirmative, active, declarative.)
2. Does Jack love Jill? (Affirmative, active, interrogative.)
3. Doesn't Jack love Jill? (Negative, active, interrogative.)
4. Jack does not love Jill. (Negative, active, declarative.)
5. Jill is loved by Jack. (Affirmative, passive, declarative.)
6. Is Jill loved by Jack? (Affirmative, passive, interrogative.)

7. Isn't Jill loved by Jack? (Negative, passive, interrogative.)
8. Jill is not loved by Jack. (Negative, passive, declarative.)

How, Bernstein asked, is musical syntax comparable to descriptive grammar?

He starts out by discarding the idea that a note can equate with a letter. Neither can a scale equate with an alphabet.

But, illustrating with Mozart's G Minor Symphony, he arrives at the following theory. He makes no claim for its philosophical exactness and calls it at best quasi-scientific.

Music		Grammar
note	=	phoneme
motif	=	morpheme (syllable such as *ma* or *si*)
phrase	=	word
section	=	clause
movement	=	sentence
piece	=	piece

Armed with such a vocabulary, Bernstein attempts to equate the primary parts of speech: noun, adjective, and verb. He equates the noun with the motif of the Mozart symphony, illustrating it on the piano (*fa mi mi, fa mi mi, fa mi mi do*). It is recognizable. It proceeds with a further phrase, which replicates the action a noun does in a declarative sentence. The motif is as recognizable as a name.

The verb is best described in music by rhythm, for rhythm is the motion in music.

The adjective or modifier is the chord. Language cannot employ the chord. The only approximation is the overtones, undertones, or associations of the single word. For language contains rhythm along one line only. This line is similar to a melodic line of music. The only equivalent would be a speaking chorus harmonizing the utterance of three different words (and three different meanings) at the same instant.

It is a literal impossibility for the human mind to comprehend the connections of literal meanings in simultaneous reception. That is why comprehensive connections and subtle meanings depend on clauses intertwining along a melodic line. Thought is sequential, accumulative.

Perhaps the writers most sympathetic are those with greatest command of modifiers: adjectives and dependent clauses. It is a command of weights and balances as well as an ear for sound overtones. For clauses do the work of chords. They qualify and describe, but not simultaneously.

Such writers as Marcel Proust, Vladimir Nabokov, Nathaniel Hawthorne, John Updike, Anthony Burgess, George Eliot, Lawrence Durrell, John Updike, Cynthia Ozick, Cormac McCarthy, Tom Wolfe, and Walt Whitman are unafraid of adjectives. The talent for adjectives involves the mounting of incongruous rather than similar ideas. Incongruity has the effect of a chord, a differentiation in meaning that is the same as differentiation in tone.

But the chord has also a function similar to a verb's. Bernstein does not expatiate on this in his lecture. It is best described by harking back to the tension of the dominant seventh, or to any chord so inconclusive it demands a resolving chord. There is a story that, because Franz Liszt slept late, a friend who wanted to talk with him came early in the morning to his house. He played a piece on the piano, stopping just before the final note, on the dominant seventh, which demands a grand, resolving final tonic. Liszt was so disturbed, listening from his bed, that he got out, ran down the stairs to the piano, and finished it. He had to. The tension in the chord demanded it.

Such tension, of course, belongs to meaning. In terms of the sentence as a grammatical unit, it would equate with a periodic sentence in the style, say, of Faulkner. A prodigious build in the beginning and middle, to be clarified, or stated, its major information withheld until the end. The following from Faulkner might be an example:

> … and he knew now what he had known as soon as he saw Hoke's this morning but had not yet thought into words: why Major de Spain had not come back, and that after this time he himself, who had had to see it one time other, would return no more.

Sentence rhythm

Despite any common vocabulary between grammar (pure meaning) and music, we are always compelled by the rhythm of sentences. Fast and slow, crescendo, diminuendo, pause, density, and rhyme dominate the meaning of a sentence and illuminate it.

The following exercises are practices in the larger rhythmical aspect of music as it applies to sentences.

Exercise 32: Sentence Permutation Fugue

Purpose: To illustrate basic structure of transformational grammar. To experiment with word rhythms and rhyme for a spoken fugue.

1. Choose a subject.
2. What do you want to say about this subject? Write a paragraph.
3. Convert subject into one simple transitive sentence in standard order. Write out the permutations of that sentence according to Noam Chomsky. When you do this, you will have every available possible permutation of its meaning as structure.
4. Choose key rhythmic words. Set down possible rhymes for them.

Example: Key Word: Yassir Arafat

Rhyming words: entrechat, Mount Ararat, smell a rat, could eat no fat

5. Use your rhyming words as alternate rhythms.

Exercise 33: Setting Sentence to Musical Background

Purpose: Observing rhythm, crescendos, diminuendos, rises, and falls.

First, do exercise eleven: Write a story, dialogue, anecdote, or stand-up comedy routine in the series of sentences listed, sticking to order and type:

Simple
Compound
Complex
Standard order
Inverted order
Interrupted sentence
Loose sentence
Periodic sentence
Parallelism
Balance
Antithesis
Gradation

Set a musical accompaniment to your piece. The musical background should fairly illustrate rises, heights, pauses, crescendos, and diminuendos. Perform (read) your piece, coordinating it with the background music (on audiotape).

The goal is not precise coordination of words to music, but rather an appropriate background of rhythm and aesthetics, an approximation.

Example:

"I Lost It in Fuquay-Varina," by Elizabeth Moose

Background Music: "It Can't Be Wrong" by Max Steiner, written for the movie *Now Voyager*, starring Bette Davis

Simple: I lost it in Fuquay Varina.
Compound: I thought, what a place in which to lose it, and I longed to have lost mine somewhere more exotic.
Complex: Mother wept when she learned of what I had lost.
Standard order: Her tears rolled after she slapped my face.
Inverted order: Had she seen the truth there, shining in my eyes?
Interrupted: She had, but she could not—since this was my first—forgive and forget it?
Loose: "You were reckless," she said, tongue-clucking and head-shaking as she rocked in housedress and scuffs, chewing on the ribbons of her frock like a cow endlessly chewing its cud in the tall wet grass of a wide pasture in the upcountry of South Carolina while green saliva began dripping out each corner of her moving mouth, landing on the floor.
Periodic: "Mother, all things, even the Ming Dynasty, the Clamshell Alliance, cream-of-wheat and Chiquita banana, even Nefertiti and Ramses II, even though they're dead, and kumquats, katydids, the Flatiron Building, Dippity-do, even prickly heat too, and Kitty Carlisle, and Bette Davis and the Beastie Boys, must change."
Balance: "Bullshit," she said, then spat out the ribbon, patted her topknot, scuffed to her bedroom, and slammed the door.
Simple: Delicacy had always marked her speech and her step.
Antithesis: Though I was hurt, I still remained proud.
Gradation: That very afternoon I left for the A & P to recapture those days when life was dark, life was sweet, life was chewy and seedy and tasty, and when, in short, there was quality in my corner, in those days, on those delectable days before I lost my Fig Newtons in Fuquay-Varina.

Exercise 34: Jargon Melody

Purpose: Inappropriate music for specialized jargon.

Select a background melody—without lyrics—and notate it, as accompaniment, for a paragraph taken from one of the following.

1. U.S. Dept. of Agriculture manual.
2. Dentistry or medical textbook.
3. Income tax form.
4. Computer instructions.
5. Rebate information form.
6. Shopping ad.
7. Directions on medicine bottle or prescription literature.

Speech sentences

What is the music of speech?

Is speech always about sentences? Do the sentences repeat? Or is speech about phrases? How tinged are speech phrases or sentences by TV speak? Jargon? Geek-speak? The illustrations of the following exercise circumscribe arcs rather than circles. They're a reminder of Stein's contention that living utterance does not have the completeness of a sentence.

Exercise 35: Overheard Conversations

Purpose: To note the difference between written and spoken language. To "hear" thematic resonance and evocation in stray dialogue.

Take a note pad with you everywhere you go so that you can take down stray conversations and lines from conversations. Eavesdrop. Listen in public places, movie lobbies, hallways, streets, dining halls, stores, and restaurants.

Write a page.

Be aware. Organize the lines in any manner you wish, but be sure they're verbatim. The snatches of conversation may be cliché, but they will evoke moods and themes. Arrange them so that they are evocative, but remain faithful to the conversation. The more specific, the better, for in the concrete lies the cosmic.

Disconnection is not a problem, for the exercise is schizophrenic.

Select and arrange lines to form a structure, a musical or thematic pattern akin to a poem.

Examples:

1. Arranged by David Poole

I'm worried.
My husband doesn't like meringue.
Like she didn't know where she was.
I don't know what to do. What does it feel like?
She'd make a Mack truck take a dirt road.
All three kids with him?
I'm trying to figure out where it is.
I wish I could.

2. Arranged by Annette Overton

The one in the pink.
Stand there, Elsie.
You could. That's easier said than done though.
Maybe she's waiting until she gets her passport.
Remember we got stuck in that horrible little town with the panama hats?

3. Arranged by Ann Wilson

Because I can see
See you sometime.
See, we used to do that.
Something-you know-silly.
Same to you.

We were all new
Argued very strongly.
That's right.

It's not going to change.
There goes one, bless her heart.

Maybe I'm blowing it up.
That's right
It's not going to change.

Bet that doesn't matter.
It's time.
Let's go.

It's been an odd year to tell the truth.
His very fixed ideas
Only 24 hours in a day.
There's a real conflict.

I wish I could get out.
I think one thing that would help.
I think it's the only way it's going to survive.
See, we used to do that
We were all new.

By getting your act together
I think you hit it.
Did you have a good time down there?
Did you get paid for doing it?

I couldn't stand it
When the normal
Surprised the hell out of me.

Is it very rough?
Well, that's what I was going to say.

Why did you apologize?
It's not going to change.
See, we used to do that.
We were all new.

It's time.
Let's go.
There goes one, bless her heart.

Formalizing speech

When speech is disconnected from the specific context that engendered it, it seems to carry great meaning. Cosmic meaning, even. That is because certain phrases stick out beyond the particular, echoing the large and vulnerable themes of humankind. This is called resonance.

Resonance is theme. Theme captured in speech rhythm is music. The undertones or overtones in speech are scarcely ever dreamed of by a speaker who has uttered words in a particular context. Most conversations dawdle along getting nowhere. Nothing is more calculated to bore than a tape recording of a party where people are having a moderately good time. It is the poets who train themselves in the art of listening with the third ear. A repetition is resonance, and the listener, not the speaker, is aware of it.

Most written language is formalized language. It is codified by print, entails convention, and communicates by category. Speech is imbedded in convention too, mostly convention worn down to cliché. But because speech is in now-time, direct and extemporaneous, it circulates with great instinct, if little thought.

Music has its conventions too. We know immediately the emotions engendered by reggae, ballad, tango, foxtrot, gypsy violin, Irish tenor, lieder, punk rock, disco, parlor songs, hip hop and rap, or old English rounds. This is the song form. Songs are born out of the notion of speech as monologue.

What is the musical form for many voices? For dialogue? In essence, there are two: the oratorio and the opera.

Oratorio

The oratorio is similar to narrated story. It is often based on retelling Biblical plots. In the great oratorios, there is usually a narrator with different singers playing (singing) the major parts (characters). But in some oratorios, there are no characters. Rather there are abstract voices singing attitudes that may be at odds or may be complementary, somewhat in the manner of the Greek chorus, or like responsive readings and chants in Protestant and Catholic churches. The oratorio form is a dynamic one in which attitudes are dramatized, or in which characters do and say (sing) a story. One thing happens, then something else happens, and another thing, etc., as E. M. Forster pointed out.

Opera

The opera is even more dynamic, and librettos notwithstanding, it contains plot (the idea of cause) as opposed to the oratorio (story). The opera is a play, the oratorio is a story. The opera involves a private drama performed on a proscenium stage. It is realistic presentation in contrast to the abstract/religious/emotional dialogue of the oratorio. And the opera was a later form.

In the opera, dramatic scenes occur with messengers bearing crucial information, with potions being drunk, quarrels being sung, love scenes being overheard, heroes being stabbed, consumptives dying, etc. Such events cause others, the drama rising to a climax in the dynamics of the play form.

The music which embody these dramatic moments are:

Duet. Two characters, often but not always lovers, conduct a dialogue in singing, alternating single melody with harmonic duet. There is a dramatic goal in every piece of music in an opera, and the duet may declare everlasting love, a plan of escape, a parting, a plot to destroy someone, etc.

Trio. Three characters conduct a three-way song involving melody and harmony. It also must have a dramatic purpose.

Quartet. Four characters conduct a four-way song involving melody and harmony, and having a dramatic goal.

Aria. A one-character burst of song dominates the opera musically, and is sung at the climatic moment, usually having been introduced in the overture, and in the first act.

Group chorus. A song in which all the principals sing, backed up by the crowds, subjects, and pawns in the drama. It often sports simultaneous trios and quartets, and acts as the finale.

Recitative. Recitative is the musical form nearest to spoken speech. It is the direct rendering of speech into a musical line. It is structured by speech rather than by music (formal melodic and harmonic patterns), and is a dialogue rather than a poem. Recitative contains the dynamic and dramatic interplay between characters, and its function is to explain or to thrust the action forward. If it is explicatory, it may lack dramatic tension. If it is the dynamic thrust of action, it is a convention.

Recitative presents a problem and a paradox. It is unacceptable to many audiences. Being formalized into music, it sounds phoney, tiresome, and ludicrous. It involves only notes and rhythm. Melodically and harmonically it is crude; we are unused to this convention. The speech is often a foreign language, and if translated, sounds silly. As explanation, it seems to go on forever. As crucial drama (a fight, a duel, a parting of the ways), it seems laughable.

Modern musical drama, the form nearest to eighteenth- and nineteenth-century opera, is the Broadway musical, and does not employ recitative. The music stops and the characters talk. The convention of recitative is thrown away. But when music stops dead and dialogue begins, there is an instantaneous diminution of dramatic tension. You have to set your mind to a world less powerful than music, the world of words. You go from high to low, from wings to earth. *West Side Story*, as if recognizing the problem, tried to institute choreography to continue the musical drama in its dramatic phases without having to jolt from musical flow to flat earth.

Formalizing speech meaning

After World War I artists proclaimed that the world of structure and reason was in shards, and that the only truthful art had to recognize the ascendancy of pieces. The center of belief and action had failed to hold, and things had fallen apart. The Dadaists, the Surrealists issued manifestos. They welcomed disorder, embraced the goal of no-meaning and artifact. Tristan Tzara wrote a "Dadaist Manifesto":

> To make a dadaist poem
> Take a newspaper
> Take a pair of scissors
> Choose an article as long as you are planning to make your poem
> Cut out the article
> Then cut out each of the words that makeup this article and put them in a bag
> Shake it gently.
> Then take out the scraps one after another in the order in which they left the bag.
> Copy conscientiously.
> The poem will be like you.

Such proclamations separating words from their reference and elevating them to a separate reality thrust literary attention toward music and other arts. Groups dedicated to surrealism, dada, and symbolism invited artists of dance, language, poetry, cinema, painting, and music to fashion a new reality and explode the old reality of conventional reference. Paul Verlaine, Stéphane Mallarmé, Luis Buñuel, Salvador Dali, André Breton, Eugene Jolas, Tristan Tzara, Paul Valéry, Man Ray, Hugo Ball, Arnold Schoenberg, Jean Cocteau, Igor Stravinsky, Gertrude Stein, Sergey Diaghilev, Andrey Bely, James Joyce, and Ernest Bloch were some of the artists collapsing the distance between music, painting, cinema, and dancing. Not a writer, composer, photographer, filmmaker, or painter remained immune. The poetics of the different movements of dada, symbolism, and surrealism waxed and ebbed as art claiming to dis-integrate also digested the revolution in ideas.

Gertrude Stein was an analyst rather than a revolutionary, and paradoxically she believed in the fixedness of character even as she tried to describe that character in process terms (continuous present tense, gerunds, and participles). Though she despised completion in syntax, she assumed the static reality of objects as true and sought only a new literary language to define them.

It is fitting to examine the correspondence of music to Stein's conversation plays to understand the possibilities of formalizing speech into music.

When you set music to speech, you can either seek to support the spirit, theme, and emotion of the content or you can seek to counter it. When the director of a play tries to give another meaning beyond or below the usual content of a line of dialogue, he refers to his motivational idea as a *subtext*. It may play against the content of the line, or it may emphasize a contemporary idea in the line. The subtext of Laurence Olivier's movie of *Hamlet*, for instance, was based on the emphatic assumption of an incestuous sexual relationship between Hamlet and his mother. The word *subtext* has become the actor's cliché.

If we were to sing an argument between two people who had crashed in traffic and dented each other's fenders, we can well imagine the climax when one sings: "I'm gonna call the cops!" and the other cries: "Go to hell, you jerk!" The recitative as opera would ascend upward with sinister threat on the "cops" line; there would be a crash of cymbals, a pause, and then a dramatic ascendance as the bass bellows "Go to" on high notes, ending with "hell" in a deep climatic note. What he would do with "you bastard" to avoid a musical anticlimax would constitute the challenge for the composer. This music would seek to support the spirit, theme, and content of the lines.

In Gilbert and Sullivan operas, the dialogue is usually complemented by the music, not countered. But it stresses a kind of nursery-rhyme rhythm in such lines as "Fastened up the handles of the big front door" so that we are charmed by its silliness. The mode is comedy; the exercise is a good humored, robust, tin-soldier, child-game; the emotions never range beyond the sentimental. It is not satire but pageantry. The singer/composer/writer/comedienne Anna Russell, on the other hand, has created musical parody of standard opera. She mimics opera from Puccini to Wagner, exaggerating the foibles of high emotion and drama to bring both low, musically and literarily. The focus of music to words in the dimension of emotion in Gilbert and Sullivan and in Anna Russell is basically fun-loving and without pretension. Gilbert and Sullivan tend to be cute. Anna Russell is analytical and good-humoredly satirical. Both make mincemeat of speech.

But it is in Gertrude Stein's word plays that we can best understand the relation of speech to music. Her later experimentation, which led her to abstraction in which not only did she split words from their meaning, but also speech sentences from a demonstrably concrete situation (her plays are not what we usually consider plays; they do not have a plot; they do not employ cause; nor are they what we usually consider poems which would translate into a simple song) brought her to nonsense by association, and to puns, homonyms, and rhymes. She disavowed the music that resulted. She was still interested only in a spatial construction of truth. She was painting words, not singing them. Yet it had the fascinating gibber of "found conversation," and she set the speeches out of context. It resulted in wit and she was rewarded. Not only did she become quotable, but she was set to music.

Virgil Thomson collaborated with her on poems. A serious musician, not extraordinarily original, but clever and accomplished, he approached the task by setting the speeches to music with American color such as hymns and folk music. He worked with her on *Four Saints in Three Acts*, and they pulled themes out of the fire like chestnuts. It had a black cast, and its spunky, beguiling music made it a hit in the 1930s. He also composed the music to *The Mother of Us All*, but Stein did not live either to hear the music or see the show.

Al Carmines, a minister of the Judson Street Church in New York, composed the music for *A Circular Play*, not in collaboration but long after Stein's death, in the 1960s. It was presented as a six-performer opera-musical, called *In Circles*, off-Broadway.

He took the play as text, mined its speeches for resonance, chose major motifs, and composed the work for singing, speaking and movement. The idea behind it is a children's game of playing circles. Its effect is incantatory, just as children's games are incantations. But he directed or focused it toward an incantation for people to dance, sing, play, be together, in circles, against all the negative forces of human life. The music is extremely derivative. It contains some gypsy violin, old-fashioned parlor music, bump and grind, Spanish flamenco, recitative mockery, Broadway lyrical, and other forms, and it is bouncy, enthusiastic, and mocking.

But in studying this musical, so bereft of plot, so basic and repetitive in theme, so banal and lifelike in its lines and phrases, there may be no better place to examine the relationship of the speech sentence to formalized music, because the speech is American English. It makes comic, but very little particular sense. It has emotion, but disconnected to any particular situation. And it leads us straight back to the child's knowledge of language as mantra. Language as the power itself when elevated to mantra.

11. Tricksters and Parodists

Larger Structures

The words *form* and *style* are often used interchangeably. For clarity, we need to distinguish between them.

Form

Form refers to shape. The *Oxford English Dictionary* gives pages of definitions of *form*, among which appear:

- A set, customary, or prescribed way of doing anything: a set method of procedure according to rule (e.g., at law); formal procedure.

- Rules, prescribed methods, formal procedure, curricula, course of exercises, parliamentary form.

- A set of fixed order of words (as used in religion), ritual; the customary or legal method of drawing up a writing or document.

- Style of expressing the thoughts and ideas in literary or musical composition, including the arrangement and order of the parts of a whole. Also method of arranging the ideas in logical reasoning; good or just order (of ideas, etc.) logical sequence.

Style

Style is the music of language that accompanies or expresses a form. The *Oxford English Dictionary* calls it a manner of writing or speaking. Here are some of the OED's definitions of style:

- The manner of expression characteristic of a particular writer (hence of an orator) or of a literary group or period; a writer's mode of expression considered in regard to clearness, effectiveness, beauty, and the like.

- Those features of literary composition which belong to form and expression rather than to the substance of the thought or matter expressed.

- A manner of discourse, or tone of speaking, adapted in addressing others or in ordinary conversation.

- A form or words, phrases or formula by which a particular idea or thought is expressed.

Form dictates style in many cases. We all know the style of Protestant church rituals that employs *thees*, *thous*, *Amens* as distinct from the style involved in a news broadcast with its jargon and such phrases as "right-wing leaders," "military coup," "international sources," "denied comment," etc. Tradition often crystallizes a style, so that the form can be recognized at once.

Although it is possible to discern style in as small a unit of prose as the sentence, it is through larger structures that we recognize it most particularly.

In this chapter, we will confine the meaning of the word *music* to the area of language style. In order to examine style, let us look at the two categories of language form we spoke of above.

Language forms of environment, behavior, and tradition

The most significant alteration of environmental and traditional forms in history has come about because of electronic communication. Where the printing press shifted emphasis to written language, radio, television, and speaking computers have brought it back to the oral. Such forms have become a worldwide environment. It is almost irrelevant whether the form fits the civilization or not.

The following list contains some of the forms of expression that pervade our Western environment, and which we recognize instantly without, perhaps, being conscious of their assumptions or style.

common prayer
pledge of allegiance
commercial
doxology
pharmacy prescriptions
Episcopal church credo
ceremony of knighthood
multiple-choice tests
church sermon
news broadcast
auction spiel
coronation ceremony
beauty pageant emcee intros

political speech
prayer and response
government forms
financial and stock-market news and reports
disk jockey patter
social work case histories
law-enforcement rules
opinion polls
law court summaries
medical diagnoses and prognoses
soap opera dialogue
law briefs
prosecuting attorneys' summaries
revivalist preachings
CB radio codes
educationists' reports and statement of objectives
parliamentary procedure
highway signs
electrical appliance instructions
debate
airport announcing
recipes
wire-services news
cocktail party introductions
packaging information on food products
pharmaceutical labeling
hospital public address information
mass transit instructions
disclaimer phrases
warning labels

The list could go on ad infinitum. There is no argument that forms have become environment. Lassitude, boredom, or ennui verges on outright irritation and malaise when we contemplate them. Yet some are holy and some ersatz, some traditional and others tradition-debased. Degradation happens when meaning is separated from form. It is like the response from the people and clerk at the checkout counter of the A & P when well-dressed Mrs. Irma Doe wheeled out her groceries saying politely "Fuck you very much," instead of "Thank you very much." The people simply did not believe what they heard, for form blots out individual authority and forbids any meaning to insinuate itself upon a customary formality.

By the same token it is often by using inappropriate content that we can perceive forms for the first time. Perhaps they are dead. Perhaps they are suddenly new. Or perhaps they are capable of what we had never dreamed.

Exercise 36: Form Exercise

Purpose: Inappropriate form for inappropriate content.

Rewrite the story of a well-known nursery rhyme similar to the two below, as if it were written by:

1. a doctor
2. a lawyer during a trial
3. a fire-and-brimstone preacher
4. a local newscaster or weatherman
5. a gossip columnist for the National Enquirer
6. a hip hop performer
7. a telemarketer

Little Miss Muffet
Sat on her tuffet
Eating her curds and whey

Along came a spider
And sat down beside her
And frightened Miss Muffet away.

Jack and Jill
Went up the hill
To fetch a pail of water.

Jack fell down
And broke his crown
And Jill came tumbling after.

Examples:

"The Heart of Muffet," a sermon by Teresa Coleman

Preacher: One fine God-sent day in the year of our Lord, 19 hundred and 34, a young woman sat on a tuffet in an open field, praise the Lord. And this little girl was called Muffet, Little Miss Muffet, because she was young in years. But she was old and black in her heart, a heart once pure and simple, Praise the Lord!

Congregation: Praise the Lord!

Preacher: She, like the adulteress in the Bible and the black-hearted Judas Iscariot, had sinned, and her transgressions were too terrible and too numerous to mention.

Congregation: Mercy!

Preacher: She, brothers and sisters, broke God's duly given laws. She worshipped her money and her tuffet and her curds and whey. She, black-hearted adulteress, thief, covetous, shameless hussy, danced on the Sabbath. God save and protect us!

Congregation: Protect us!

Preacher: He sent upon this Muffet a plague in the form of one of his most horrible creatures: a plague of eight legs, to set her back on the road to righteousness. This plague was not unlike the plagues He sent to the Egyptians. And you sinners here today are due a few plagues. And they'll sit down beside you and they will put the fear of God in your heart!

Congregation: Amen!

Preacher: And you'll quake and tremble and try to run away like Muffet, but, brothers and sisters, you cannot escape the terrible wrath of God!

Congregation: Oh Lord!

Preacher: Now is the time to cast aside your sinful tuffets of luxury—

Congregation: Amen!

Preacher: Your curds and your sinful wheys!

Congregation: Tell it, Preacher! Amen!

Exercise 37: Multiple Choice Poem

Write a multiple choice poem.

Examples:

"To My Poopsie," by Katy Munger

To my (A) poopsie, (B) sweetums, (C) honey
You're not (A) cute (B) rich (C) funny
It's been all (A) summer (B) winter (C) fall
And you don't (A) come (B) write (C) call

I've been (A) hook-winked (B) dumped on (C) bewitched
And you're an (A) monster (B) dog (C) bitch
You made me (A) sorry (B) fat (C) drunk
You're an (A) tease (B) rat (C) skunk
You taught me (A) laughter (B) lust (C) love
You left me (D) none of the above.

Literary forms

Voice and style are related. Style is literary music. Voice is the mark of a particular author. Literature is the art of self-expression when it has become a communication. Presumably, because content finds its form, it offers an escape and reassurance against the hegemony of forms of environment, behavior, and tradition. But so ubiquitous are they that literature is under their sway.

Is a person born with his own voice? The serious writer or "artist" Ezra Pound defined as *inventors* those who found a new process, or whose extant work gives us the first known example of a process, and as *masters* those who combined a number of such processes, and who used them as well or better than the inventors.

Inasmuch as we learn language itself, we are imitators, because it is difficult to grasp the pattern of one's essential uniqueness, let alone express it. All beginning writers imitate.

Authenticity of content illumined by integrity of style is the distinctive mark of a writer. Voice is evident in style, and style cannot be separated from content. The substance of a man's particular formation of psyche is expressed in style. Ezra Pound called style "charged language." The method of achieving it was threefold:

- **Phanopoeia.** Throwing the object (fixed or moving) onto the visual imagination. Use of images.

- **Melopoeia.** Inducing emotional correlations by the sound and rhythm of the speech. Use of sound and rhythm.

- **Logopoeia.** Inducing both of the effects by stimulating the associations (intellectual or emotional) that have remained in the receiver's consciousness in relation to the actual words or word groups employed. Linguistic. The use of both image and sound in syntactical reference.

There are many literary forms, but the major configurations resolve into poetry, prose, and perhaps scripts for theater, movie, or TV.

Strict forms in literature: Poetry

Traditional education used to be based on memorization and the practice of strict forms. Little emphasis was placed on original thinking, even less on the content of forms students were made to master. Strict rhythm, beat, and rhyme were the goal of novice pupil-writers, and the literary forms of verse were drummed into their heads through large-passage memorization.

With concentration, it is not hard to memorize chapter and verse. Beat and rhythm make it easier. How often have people remembered the number of days in each month by the verse:

> Thirty days hath September
> April, June, and November
> All the rest have thirty-one
> Excepting February alone.

Rhythm and rhyme enabled the intellectual part of the memory to rest.

Such mindlessness in the face of beat and rhythm is apparent in the elementary transpositions of some famous verse into Christmas carols.

To the tune "Here We Go a-Carolling":

> Because I could not stop for Death
> He kindly stopped for me
> The carriage held but just ourselves
> And Immortality
> We slowly drove—He knew no haste
> And I had put away
> My labor and my leisure too
> For his Civility.
>
> —Emily Dickinson

To the tune "Deck the Halls":

> I hold it true, whate'er befall
> Fa-la-la-la-la, la-la-la-la.
> I feel it when I sorrow most
> Fa-la-la-la-la, la-la-la-la.
> 'Tis better to have loved and lost
> Fa-la-la-la-la-la-la-la-la.

Then never to have loved at all
Fa-la-la-la-la-la-la-la-la.

Such prowess, like children's games, delights because it is parody. The words flout. Pure music contains the word message, and either the Christmas emotion is banalized, or the subject is subsumed in the cliché of Christmas emotion.

Metered poetry shares the strictness of music. The following parodies demonstrate the transposition of substance to familiar forms. The content is entirely subordinated to the form. We are left only with admiration for the cleverness of word manipulators. It is crude flirtation in the realm of strict form.

Excerpt of a Parody by Frank Jacobs from *Mad Magazine*

If Poe's "The Raven" were written by Joyce Kilmer

I think that I shall never hear
A raven who is more sincere …
A raven who repeats his words
Until I think I'm for the birds …

It is no wonder that twentieth century innovators were obliged to throw out beat and rhyme. Ezra Pound as a poet sought the new in speech. John Dewey and the twentieth-century literary experimenters threw out memory and beat for process. In rebellion, they pondered speech patterns, simple condensation, or random placement of words. They wanted to create "new artifacts" and to discover new rhythms.

Beat and rhyme were left to the advertisers. Unusable for serious statement, they were perfected for hawking aspirin and beauty lotions.

But they reappear. As Alfred Dorn declares the sonnet dead, and others, the demise of the novel, sonnets and novels crop up in new forms. Dr. Seuss is Mother Goose recast. *A Star is Born* and *Little Women* are novels remade time and again as movies. Many poets practice the sonnet form not only to defy critics, but in an attempt to incorporate contemporary experience into tradition, an individuation devoted to integration. Collective content may survive change through form.

Exercise 38: The Sonnet

Purpose: To practice iambic pentameter and set cadence.

Choose five sonnets by Shakespeare and read them aloud until you drive people crazy. Drench yourself in iambic pentameter. It will make the language form itself around you in that shape.

Write a modern sonnet, each of whose fourteen lines ends in some form/tense of the same common verb. The more common the verb, the easier the sonnet will be to construct. Do not use archaic language. Give the sonnet authentic content; don't just use the form to say nothing, to do a boring, gutless exercise. Say something you want to say. The iambics may be broken up, but keep them true to beat.

Examples:

"Poetry in the Quad," by Kit Fitzsimmons

> Descartes once said, "I think, therefore I am."
> And who am I to question what I am
> Supposed to take from that? I mean, I *am*
> A mere Creative Writing student. Am
> I thinking? Am I being who I am,
> Or is this sonnet an assignment? Am
> I drifting, waning, writing nothing? Am
> I waxing Ars Poetical? I am!
> I am! I am! I am! I am! I am!
> Two beats or not two beats? That's all iamb.
> And see? What's worse, I've punned the word 'iamb'!
> I am iambic, but as such I am
> Now inundated with a pulse. I. Am.
> I think; therefore, I do not give a damn.

"Will You Run With Me?" by Mary Jo Southern

> So "Will you run with me?" he said. We ran
> a race, not knowing thoughts would also run
> through sweaty heads: but then I ran
> some errands, running into him; chills ran
> right down my spine; how I did want to run
> so far away and hide my frosted head; get run
> right over; since I thought this lovely tune that ran
> in my head was not in his; I got so run
> down, I ate a plate of liver, so I could run
> right fast for respect; it all ran

fine. On life's piano, how we ran
the scales in harmony! Then I began to run
his life. He ran me out. I would have run
my car into a pole; but I watched my new hose run.

"A Stirring Sonnet," by Brandon Proia

You gave up all your internships to stir
apocalypses of the starving, stir,
foment revolt. As for me, all I stir
is stirred with spoons. Me, leftist boyfriend, stir-
frying, full-time, at home. Your stomach stirs
as you teach Marx in parks, and thoughts are stirred
toward me—the revolution in me stirred
to feed you only, calm you when you stir
from sleepy nightmares. You beckon, stirring
the air in circles with your arms, to stir
unfed masses; you offer them my stir-
fry, endless bowlfuls, and beg them rise, stir
up trouble in the streets; they never stirred,
their stomachs empty, hearts we could not stir.

Exercise 39: Switching Literary Forms

Exercise: Convert the following speech of Vershinin from *The Three Sisters* by
Anton Chekhov into

1. a Mother Goose rhyme or limerick or Dr. Seuss poem
2. a Hemingway or Gertrude Stein dialogue
3. a Faulkner paragraph
4. a dramatic narrative as rewritten by Henry James, Jane Austen, Emily
Dickenson, e.e.cummings, Flannery O'Connor, Charles Dickens.

Be as free as you want with the speech even if you distort. The point is to make it
true in feeling and style of the writer you are mimicking.

I often wonder: suppose we could begin life over again, knowing what we were
doing? Suppose we could use one life, already ended as a sort of rough draft for
another? I think that every one of us would try, more than anything else, not to
repeat himself, at the very least he would rearrange his manner of life, he would
make sure of rooms like these, with flowers and light ... I have a wife and two

daughters, my wife's health is delicate and so on and so on, and if I had to begin life all over again I would not marry ... No, no!

Examples

"I Do Not Like This Life of Mine" (based on the well-known nursery rhyme "I Do Not Like Thee Dr. Fell")

I do not like this life of mine
I do not think it's very fine
I hate it more than garden peas
I'd like a new one if you please.

I'd like this one as a rough draft
I'd like it if it were not aft
I'd like it if it came before
And then was gone and was no more.

Yes, I'd like it if it could be changed
If all of it were rearranged
And if I didn't have a wife
Oh, that would surely be a life.

Another limerick version:

If I could start over with life,
I wouldn't consider the knife,
But remain as a bachelor
Which would be more naturaler
Than trying to put up with a wife!

"I'd Change It All," à la Hemingway, by Mark Meares

Nick was getting married in two days. He had promised Maria that he would meet her at the station and they would go to Malapunta. He felt bad about leaving Bill. Bill would not understand why he had to go and would be very hurt.

"Do you ever think about a second chance in life," he asked.

"Sure," Bill said.

"What would you do?"

"I'd do it all."

"Would you change anything?"

"I'd change it all," Bill said.

"There would have to be something you wouldn't want to change," Nick said.

"Nope."

"How about your family?"

"Least of all them. I'd never marry."

Nick was angry. Bill was taking a cheap shot. Manuel had probably already told him about Maria.

Bill got up. "I must go. Some of us have a war to fight." Nick started to hit him.

"Goodbye, Bill. Someday soon you will know death and want to live again."

"You and your bloody death," Bill said, turning his back and walking away.

Nick put his face in his hands. No, he would not die again. Never. It was a one-time thing and he knew that it was useless to think about it. But there had been nights when you had died, nights long and dark when you would light matches to keep you from dying, trying to shut out the fire bombs cracking far away but always too close for comfort. But you would die anyway, would feel your whole body get up from the cot and run away. But then there was always morning and you would feel the sun hot in the cold morning air and your body would be there and you were no longer scared. But that was not death. Not the death you had seen one night in Madrid, a young boy's face white like the belly of a dead fish, gone blank facing the firing squad of Loyalist soldiers. Not the death your father had made you look at and told you was his mother. No, you had never really died; but if you would feel it for just one instant and then live again, you might never want to do it again.

Loose forms in literature: Prose

Prose, despite formalities of syntax, suggests a more random composition than, say, metered verse. When a writer is familiar with words, his sentences, paragraphs, and language tight-fitting as kidskin gloves, he has correlated his inner rhythms of breath and heartbeat with those of his expression. In the cosmos of reading and communication, we know this as style. When the form is loose, individuation is understood by style. The beat, the mantra is there, but it is not evident. It may not even be definable by the writer himself. But it is there.

Readers and critics of prose define in terms of content or substance. But since content in the medium of reading cannot be separated from its expression, language must be reckoned with.

We may perceive this relationship in terms of the old Platonic question: "Do you know something if you can't say it? Do you understand something if you can't write it?"

Imitation

We have seen that beginning writing is always imitation. How much better then to be conscious in imitation. Many practiced writers set out that way—Benjamin Franklin did with the *Spectator*:

> About this time I met with an odd volume of the *Spectator*. It was the third. I had never before seen any of them. I bought it, read it over and over, and was much delighted with it. I thought the writing excellent, and wished, if possible, to imitate it. With that view I took some of the papers, and making short hints of the sentiment in each sentence, laid them by a few days, and then without looking at the book, tried to complete the papers again, by expressing each hinted sentiment at length and as fully as it had been expressed before, in any suitable words that should come to hand. Then I compared my *Spectator* with the original, discovered some of my faults and corrected them. (*Autobiography* 1771-1790)

The fact that Franklin derived a style from imitating subject matter, or expressing the same content (sentiment), is important. It was not that he was trying consciously to ape a style for a different content. He was assuming that the truth of the content demanded an ideal style.

We all read for truth. The ideal reader wants to know what the book says about how he should live or what life means. The process of reading involves recognition either at once or at last. If the recognition is at last, it is the recognition, as Plato says through Socrates, of what we knew all along but didn't know we knew.

We do not need to become bogged down in this dilemma, but we do need to know that there is one. For writing seriously ultimately involves expressing your truth. And when we are influenced by the truths we recognize in writers who mean much to us, our truth and our expression are not separated from theirs.

In imitating styles, it is advisable to choose a writer whom you love—certainly not one to whom you remain indifferent. If you copy a paragraph from a writer whom you like, you are for the first time aware of the style. You have scanned it before. Now you hear it. Read it aloud and you understand its sweep and the way its clauses and phrases contribute to its effect. It is a process connected with the understanding you derived from practicing the types of sentences in chapter 4, exercise 11, and syllable-izing a sentence in chapter 10, exercise 31.

If you try selective imitation, it will mean expressing the same subject matter, as Ben Franklin did, putting down the writer's ideas and then rewriting by memory. Or you may choose a new subject that corresponds to the original and then write it in the style of the original.

It is helpful first to analyze the style, its peculiarities, assumptions, and methods, before you begin to mimic. Look at the composition of the sentences, the figures of speech, the open ideas, and hidden assumptions under the prose.

Exercise 40: Style Analysis

Make an analysis of the style of an author you like.

Consider:

Sentence structure and syntax
Tone
Word usage
Figures of speech
Organization
Attitudes or ways of thinking and perceiving

Examples:

Analysis of J. D. Salinger, by David Krinsky

Syntax: Salinger uses long, complex sentences. Most sentences digress with extensive use of commas and parentheses to set off subordinate ideas.

Words: He often uses abstract words and he interprets them through the use of figures of speech. He is also very colloquial.

Figures of Speech: He uses metaphors and similes extensively. For example: he likens Zooey to a tour of a steamship led by him in an old Jantzen bathing suit.

Organization: Salinger seems to lack organization, but uses temporal methods. He often uses letters to provide background material. He likes to get philosophical and often quotes Eastern religion and great Western writers.

Subject Matter: Salinger uses very ordinary situations but enlivens them with fascinating, highly intellectual, and articulate characters. He deals with bright, romantic, and despairing adolescents who study their own struggle to make sense of their lives.

Attitude: He is subjective and opinionated. He gets personal with the reader and guides him along. He often contradicts himself, and qualifies in the extreme. For example: "Her fingers, though trembling, or because they were trembling."

Analysis of A. A. Milne, by Virginia Hege

Sentence Structure: Milne tends to use compound sentences, particularly when describing actions or thought processes, in which case the compound sentence is really a series of sentences strung together with coordinating conjunctions. In contrast to these exceedingly long narrative sentences, his dialogue often consists of very short single-sentence or single-word exchanges.

Tone: Milne's characters speak and think in the loftiest tone imaginable, assuming themselves experts on any subject at hand and speaking with the pomp of a seasoned professor. Milne carries this tone throughout his narration, which is utterly formal.

Word Usage: Characteristic of Milne is the Capitalized Word. Milne frequently capitalizes ordinary words, spotlighting the words appropriate to each character. This capitalization adds to the formality of the prose by making simple adjectives into profound pronouncements and common nouns into institutions as established and revered as the Holy Bible or the United States of America. Milne also employs unusual modifiers, using common nouns and verbs as adjectives: "an exercising sort of way," "a very particular morning thing."

Figures of Speech: Personification abounds: apart from the obvious example of the animals themselves, Milne's general narration contains the personification common to children's literature. "Little soft clouds played happily in a blue sky ...

Subject Matter: In the manner of the mock-heroic, Milne places his characters in the most absurd situations—trapping a Heffalump, for instance—and treats them as situations of most dire consequence.

Exercise 41: Imitation

Write an imitation of a writer whom you like.

Example:

"Like Looking," an imitation of A. A. Milne, by Melanie Sumner

> "You aren't listening," he said, looking very sour and prickly. She hummed to herself because humming is such a nice sound, not like burping which is not a very nice sound.
>
> "It wasn't exactly listening," she said. "It was more like looking. I was looking."
>
> He still looked rather sour, but not as prickly.
>
> She continued thoughtfully. "Well, of course looking isn't at all like listening, but I think looking and listening rather like each other and want to do the same sort of thing."
>
> He didn't think so.
>
> She began to think that he would always be prickly, and since it wasn't a bad sort of prickly, rather the soft fuzzy kind of prickly that comes on peaches, she didn't mind and went on humming to herself.

Parody

Parody, the word, derives from the Greek *parodia*, meaning a burlesque poem or song. According to the *Oxford English Dictionary*, it is a composition in which the characteristic turns of thought and phrase of an author are mimicked and made to appear ridiculous, especially by applying them to ludicrously inappropriate subjects.

The purest parody is accomplished by exaggeration of the most serious features, themes, characters, or atmospheres of a writer. It is taking the sacrosanct to extreme lengths. Duncan Smith parodies Faulkner's themes of old maids, Southern grotesques, forgotten aristocrats, etc. by exaggerating his very recognizable Biblical style, replete with loose and endless run-on clauses imbedded in his periodic sentences:

> Janie was not the first to die at Ellis House. Both of her old maid sisters, Ida and Mrs. Gay, who could really not be considered an old maid because she had been married; not married in the way most girls dream of, with the church wedding, the Baptist minister, the flowers and the white gown, even though she had all of these; but married in the way most wealthy girls with plain faces are: to a very tall and handsome man (in this instance, to the very tall, mustached, and witty Mr. Robert Gay, who, after the ceremony, ravished her once, took her money, and then drank himself through it to his death) had died.

Another way of parody, more calculated and less pure, is the application of opposite subject matter to the style of a particular author. The following spoof of Henry James contrasts the subject matter of the *Dick and Jane Readers* with James's theme of American family relationships.

"The Henry James Reader," by Clay Carmichael

> Dick was the younger of the children, and was usually thought of as the taller, the classification being in general that Jane was the shorter. Spot, however tall, and to his deep chagrin, was still only a dog and brilliant at it, although our story is chiefly concerned with Dick and Jane, suffice it to say that he was a dog and moreover, as people said, a tall dog, even though there were taller dogs to be found in Dick and Jane's neighborhood.

> Dick and Jane were about to take a trip which would astonish all their friends and displease a great many of them—What might they call it so that they might not misinterpret their words?—a trip onto the lawn of their suburban home, on which Spot, running after a polished, maroon ball, decided was the lovely beginning of a splendid winter morning.

The following example, based on an incident of suicide death by a middle-aged woman jumping out of a fifth-floor window, demonstrates the styles and attitudes of Flannery O'Connor.

"Jumping from the Fifth Floor"

Flannery O'Connor, by Larry Kirkland

When Mrs. Edwards finished blanching and canning her string beans that morning and decided to drive into town to see what she might pick up on sale, the last thing she expected to see was a half naked woman perched on the windowsill on the fifth floor of the new Holiday Inn. But there she was, half naked and as big as life. She pulled the car off the highway behind a pick up truck loaded down with half a dozen colored field hands and two sacks of feed. Up ahead were two or three police cars with blue lights flashing.

Mrs. Edwards cupped her hand over her eyes and looked up at the woman. Lord, it was hot, so hot in fact that she considered taking off her sneakers and putting them in the car, but she decided against it since she had never particularly liked the image of herself getting around flat bare-foot.

The woman was fat, that much Mrs. Edwards could tell without her glasses, her breasts resting on her pot belly. For a moment that woman seemed to be ready to jump. Mrs. Edwards gasped loudly and one of the colored field hands on the truck cried, "There she blows." But she didn't jump. Instead she threw herself against the wall and let out a scream that could be heard all the way out to the highway.

"Well, I'll be damned, "Mrs. Edwards muttered to herself. She watched as the policeman crawled out on the ledge and hauled her back inside.

The colored people were laughing now. But Mrs. Edwards didn't think it was funny at all. She thought it was disgusting—just plain disgusting that a white woman would bare her breasts before anyone who might care to look—especially Negroes. It was disgusting for her to get everybody all worked up and then not to go through with it.

"Trash," she said aloud, "worse than coloreds any day."

Exercise 42: Parody

Write a parody of no more than one page of a writer whom you hate or love and who has a pronounced style.

Make an analysis of the style as in exercise 40.

Use a specific situation related to the themes, characters, and plot characteristic of your author. The parody will work best if you keep your author's content in mind.

Your theme and plot should be similar to the author's—or it should be absolutely incongruous.

Exercise 43: Parody with Given Situation

Write a parody of no more than one page of one of the following:

Henry James (Specify which story or novel)
Marcel Proust (Scott-Moncrieff translation)
Virginia Woolf
Anton Chekhov
Charles Dickens
Edgar Allen Poe
William Shakespeare
Donald Barthelme
Jonathan Swift
Norman Mailer
Laurence Durrell
Anaïs Nin
J. D. Salinger
D.H. Lawrence
Walt Whitman
Ernest Hemingway
e.e. cummings
Gabriel Garcia Marquez
Franz Kafka
Mark Twain
Toni Morrison
Allen Ginsberg
James Baldwin, etc.

Base the parody on one of the following:

1. applying for unemployment insurance
2. catching your husband or wife with another
3. one of the following fairy tales

> Humpty Dumpty
> Red Riding Hood
> Beauty and the Beast
> Jack and the Beanstalk
> Cinderella
> The Three Little Pigs
> Rapunzel
> Snow White and the Seven Dwarfs
> Rumpelstiltzskin
> The Little Mermaid
> The Little Matchstick Girl

4. an incident in a church
5. an incident on a picnic involving guilt and a love triangle.
6. watching a fat woman threatening to commit suicide by jumping out of the ninth story of a hotel.
7. shopping for groceries
8. auditioning for the TV show American Idol

Examples: "Emily Dickinson in Line for Unemployment," by Terry Bruns

> I'm an English Major! Who are you?
> Are you—an English Major—too?
> Then there's a lot of us?
> Oh hell! We're ubiquitous—you know!
>
> But how dreary—to be—practical!
> How ungainful—how mundane—
> To know of science—math and stuff
> And other things arcane!

"Howl for Humpty Dumpty," an Allen Ginsberg parody by Whitney Ward

> I have seen the best minds of my generation
> Falling, hysterical, cracking, scrambled, mad ...

Destroyed by height, by expectation and carrying the weight of the
world, he fell.

And where were you, Walt Whitman?
Too busy stroking your beard and dragging your bare feet
through the lilacs to hear the Howl, the shrill "great cry" he
gave before the tumultuous fall into despairing, dark, angelic down-
ward …

Did you eye the paramedics in their crisp, white uniforms—
the king's horses and men that carried him off?

Were they trying to pick up the eggshell pieces of a world that
Will never be right or "together again?"

Ultimately we can examine the expression of the individual (style and voice) better
in large units of prose than in any other form. Parody is the best display window,
being the sincerest form of flattery.

12. Rhythm Is Meaning

Meaning and rhythm

Shakespeare put into our thoughts the possibility of "a tale told by an idiot … signifying nothing," and contemporary play directors seized upon it as the perfect metaphor for our times. Such is the modern day faith in meaninglessness that we have accepted its consequence, despair.

Can there be such a thing as a tale signifying nothing? Any tale spoken aloud, even by an idiot, has sound and rhythm—music. But music does not have to *mean*. In music, there are five basic elements:

1. form
2. harmony
3. melody
4. tone color
5. rhythm

Every sound has rhythm varying from the barely perceptible to the rigorous, from the loose to the strict. There is stress, accent, or beat.

What is rhythm? How do we know it?

It is the breaking up of the element of *time* with *motion,* or a sense of motion. Life is sustained in the rhythms of heartbeat, blood, breathing, walking, jumping, swimming, and dancing. These rhythms are not separate from the rhythms of manifest nature, the cycling of the sun, the phases of the moon, orbital patterns, ocean waves, seasons, etc.

Heartbeats occur in pairs, one accented, the other unaccented. Breathing can be considered rhythmically similar, inhalation being accented, exhalation unaccented.

The ocean's waves beat against shore with the climax of the seventh wave. In music, there developed the pattern of the musical scale of seven notes within the octave. The chords based on each note offered the conception of the dominant-seventh chord because it demanded resolution in the dominant-one chord, foundation of the octave. The passage of the moon is the passage of blood in the menstrual cycle of women, connected with the tides, with the seven days of the week, the multiples of seven forming the twenty-eight-day cycle that is the shape of time as we know it in the moon calendar and the word *month*, which names it. Seven also are the colors of the prism seen in the reflection of sun through water, the rainbow. There are three primary colors, red, blue, and yellow, whose interstices mix to form the four additional colors, orange, brown, green, and purple.

The relationship between words and music

Similarities

1. Sounds in both words and music rely on *timing* to achieve an emotional effect. For instance, increased speed in music causes increased excitement just as shorter sentences heighten an emotional effect in speech.

2. A rise in the *pitch* of speech gives increased tension. So does a rise in tone in melody. The loudness or softness of tone in speech and in music has similar affects on people.

3. A melody can be exact in approximating vocal speech. For complete faithfulness, the vocal line has to preserve the natural stress of every syllable at every point. This is not only possible: it is the given of song.

Dissimilarities

1. Speech words have a more complex rhythm than music.

2. Form-based music has a regular, recurring beat. Words, when they are set to music, must fit into this recurring beat. This makes music the master. Some word syllables are held onto beyond their normal speech length. Usually words are sung much slower than they would be spoken in natural speech. Rap and hip hop may be exceptions. In every case, the needs of music, with its strict beat and measures, subjugates words in their referential aspect.

3. Vowels have more value in vocal music than consonants. Plosive or unvoiced consonants are virtually worthless. You can't sing *d*, *t*, or *p*. And the affricative hisses and buzzes of *s* or *z*, and the humming, nasal affricatives such as *m*, *n*, or *ng* are little better.

4. Philosophically, words and music perform different functions. Sentences go forward to fulfill a narrative or intellectual idea. Words reference meanings that individual notes do not. Music is based on repetition of motifs, fragments of

phrases. In language, repetition confuses, bores, and irritates. The realm of reference must change, and the ideas or narrative must expand.

5. The color of the tone of voice or musical instrument has effect on meaning. Music provides only the color, not the intellectual meaning. If somebody says hateful words to a baby in a crooning, tender voice: "I loathe you, Rosemary's Baby. You are evil! May you rot in hell where a rat will come at midnight and chew off your nose!" the baby may gurgle in response. He may coo to the love-sound, not knowing the meaning. The real content is disguised, betrayed. Emotional color substitutes for literal reference. Music prevails.

Musical divisions: beat, measure, accent, tempo

Beat

Musical beat is associated with heartbeats, of which there are approximately seventy-two per minute. *Beat refers to the time value of a sound or note.* Notes can be divided into six in their usual usage. The most common is the **quarter note**. It is counted as one beat. A **half note** is two beats. A **dotted half note** is three beats. A **whole note** is four beats.

But we may divide the quarter note into shorter intervals. We can do two beats in the time we do the quarter note, and this will show us the interval of an eighth note. Divide that in half and we have the sixteenth note, in which there are four beats to a quarter. Half of that is the thirty-second note, of which there are eight beats to a quarter. Rests equate silences with the value of these notes. There are whole, half, quarter, eighth, sixteenth, and thirty-second rests. A *dot (.)* written after a note or a rest increases its length by one half.

Measure

The grouping of beats into equal parts is called *measure.* The beginning of rhythmic distinction begins with the measure because there is a difference in the force of the beats, and the awareness of this difference causes the grouping. Some beats are light; some are heavy.

There are two basic grouping of beats, a group that contains two units, called *duple meter*, and a group of three beats called *triple meter*.

In prosody the basic accentuated feet are known as *iamb, trochee, anapest, dactyl* and *spondee.*

Iambic: U _ U _ U _   The curfew tolls the knell of parting day.

Trochaic: _ U _ U _ U   Tell me not in mournful numbers.

Anapest: UU_UU_UU_ His cohorts were gleaming in purple and gold.

Dactylic: _ _U_ _U_ _   One man, unfortunate, weary of breath.

Spondee: _ _ _ _ _ _   See-saw, see-saw, fall off, hee-haw.

Duple meter in music corresponds to iambic or trochaic verse. That is, its flow contains a succession of beats or pulses that fall into a measure of two beats, one strongly accented, the other unaccented. This is a replica of our heartbeat. In the following, the trochaic "Twinkle Twinkle, Little Star" divides into 2/4 time, into measures with two beats each:

> Twinkle, twinkle, little star,
> How I wonder what you are.

The verse "Frere Jacques" also falls into duple meter, but since the phrase "Frere Jacques" takes four syllables to complete its thought rather than two (like "Twinkle"), it might be more natural to express it musically as 4/4 time rather than 2/4.

> Frere Jacques
> Frere Jacques
> Dormez-vous?
> Dormez-vous?

The following lines from Longfellow's "Hiawatha" could also be written as 4/4, or 2/4, but perhaps are more naturally in 4/4 time.

> Listen to the Indian Legend, to the tale of Hiawatha.
> But the fearless Hiawatha Heeded not her woman's warning.

The choice of 2/4 or 4/4 time is usually decided by how many beats it takes to complete a phrase.

Triple meter corresponds to either anapest or dactylic feet. The following lines are examples of this 3/4 time.

> One Man unfortunate, weary of breath
> And the voice of the nightingale never is mute
> Oh, say can you see by the dawn's early light

The words of the national anthem fall into anapests with three beats, an accented and two weaker ones.

> Oh, say can you see by the dawn's early light

In the musical version, there is a manipulation of the duration of certain syllables. The word-syllable *see*, for instance, is held for two beats. Nevertheless, the time is unequivocally triple meter (3/4 time).

In the following, the syllables also fall into triple meter:

> Kentish Sir Byng stood for his king
> Bidding the crop-headed parliament swing
> March them along, fifty-score strong
> Stout-hearted gentlemen, singing this song.

Although this could be expressed as 3/4 time, the quicker tempo might find its way into music in terms of eighth notes, and would be rendered as 6/8 time.

The mathematical distribution of notes within a measure. There are three processes by which time can be manipulated within a measure. There are **augmentation, diminution,** and **stretto**.

A motif may be played, assigning different intervals of time, either shorter or longer, to each note. One instrument opposes a second instrument, each playing the same tune, but coordinating it to a different time scheme. The motif is played against itself. Such technique is the basis of the fugue, the madrigal, and the round. By holding a note (doubling or tripling the time) or by shortening it (halving, thirding, or quartering the time), the rhythmical pattern of the motif is modified by variation and complication.

Augmentation means increasing the time value in each note of the motif, thus extending it—that is, changing it.

Diminution means shortening the duration of each note in the theme, thus changing it.

Stretto is the practice of overlapping one theme with another. The beginning note of a motif may be repeated by a second part very shortly after the first part has begun. This is what happens in a round like—"Three Blind Mice." Many fugues end with this practice.

Compound measures: In regular measures of duple or triple meter, the accent falls on the first note or syllable. We have seen the relationship of 4/4 time and

2/4 time, but 4/4 is still reducible to duple meter, for the third beat may not be as stressed as the first, but it still gets more emphasis than the second or fourth beat.

The most common measures other than 2/4, 3/4, or 4/4 are 6/8, 6/4, 9/8, or 12/16. But every one of these is reducible to duple meter or triple meter, being based on multiples of two or three.

Accent

In regular rhythm, the accent falls on the first beat of a measure. But interest is generated when rhythms become irregular. When stress is shifted from its legitimate, expected location, there is a sense of complication, excitement, or daring. In complicated rhythm schemes, composers play two notes against three. This is easy enough, for the second note of a duplet falls exactly between the second and third note of a triplet. But if you play three against four, three against five, or three against eight, it is more difficult and becomes subject to interpretation.

Tempo

Tempo refers to the pace at which a piece is played, the rate of speed of the beats. The faster the succession of beats the faster the tempo, and the slower the succession the slower the tempo. The tempo of a piece of music affects the total emotion. Composers give stage directions for tempo, such as *andante, allegro*, etc.

The arithmetic of song: Syllables on beat

Measure is stringent. It has no ambiguity. It was the basis for truth as postulated by the ancients until Pythagoras, and the view of the world was formulated in musical terms by the laws of the sun and the moon. Philosophers were not what we usually think of as philosophers, but musicians, experimenters, and explorers of number and vibration as coordinated by season and elements.

In song, the question is not which is more important: words or music. They come together, making song the most universal musical form. The meaning of the words breaks free of the medium of language into the medium of sound and one step further into the medium of music. This is not a new dimension, but a return to the dimension from which words may have come. For meaning in language is not conceived apart from tone and rhythm. It is conceived *in* them. Song is the ultimate unity of words and rhythm, in which the words *are* the melody, and in which the shape, a monologue of one sentiment, *is* the sentiment.

Exercise 44: Word Composition to Instrumental Music—Solo

Purpose: Coordination of rhythms/Write words to music:

1. Choice of music. Pick something instrumental and in the public domain.

2. Find the music first. You may conceive of the idea before the music. You may want to parody the music, writing words incongruous to the musical idea, or you may want to implement or illustrate the musical idea. Or there are countless intermediate possibilities.

3. The words may be sense or nonsense, but they must fit the measured beat. But try not to follow exactly the melodic line. Try to vary the word rhythm with the rhythm of the melodic line. Write against the beat.

4. Notate exactly to measure. The words must be able to be read exactly, and not to be able to be interpreted. It must match, beat to beat, syllable to syllable, identically, so that it can be rendered the same way every time it is performed.

Example: The following excerpt is from a much longer work. If one has access to or familiarity with the music accompaniment cited, one might try singing a few measures, matching syllables to beats. In performance, however, the words are *spoken*, not sung.

"Windy, Wary Fairies"

Music: Bach, Brandenburg Concerto no. 27
Words: Clay Carmichael

> In the town where the man
> and his little brother ran
> by the sea
> and they danced on the plants
> and the windy wary fairies
> and the farmers in their dairies
> and they rattle on their drums
> made of oranges and plums
> and the sky revel red
> grabs a fairy by her head
> and the little goblins run
> in a circle in the sun
> and the blue lassie laughs
> when the cows come home

and the stars glitter out
and they wander all around
then the sky burned black
when the night comes on
and the nightgowns cry
but the windy wary fairies
wade in water by the lake
and they revel and they rattle
and they rabble through the night
till the elves come out
and the trolls always fight
and they fight and they fight
over picky little things
in the middle of the night
and the red toads laugh till the sun rise comes
and the windy wary fairies in a ravel round the moon
and they revel rabble revel
to a mushroom tune
but the trolls don't laugh
when their warts grow back
and the squirrels do a jig
and they jabber and they jabber
and they jabber and they jabber jabber jabber
till the jab runs out

Rhythm as attention

Ultimately meaning is rhythmic recognition.

When the pulses are taken charge of consciously and maneuvered into fixed beat we have entered the realm of mathematical rhythm. We need only percussion. We can dispense with melody and harmony, and even tone, the other elements of music.

Songs, as we have seen, use words in conventional syntax aligned with melody, harmony, and rhythm of either duple or triple meter. But in using rhythm to illuminate language, we can do away with intermediaries. We can do away with melody. We can do away with harmony. We can do away with syntax, (i.e., sentences). We can combine percussive rhythm with words alone, words outside the framework of syntax. What happens is that attention is focused on the word alone, and the meaning or reference of that word is penetrated. We are back in the precincts of repetition as a method of perceiving the essence of a word. It is like repeating the word *butter* fifteen times or until it loses its referential meaning. As a word it is trochaic, and therefore duple meter. Beat it out percussively, chant it, and you may have a meaning that goes far beyond its referential meaning.

Speak aloud to the rhythm of "Frère Jacques" the following imitation of Gertrude Stein's valentine to Sherwood Anderson:

John Dos Passos
John Dos Passos

Gertrude Stein
Gertrude Stein

Lawrence Ferlinghetti
Lawrence Ferlinghetti

Valentine,
Please be mine.

This is a witty placing of attention on great American writers by rhythm rather than reference. It is a sophisticated notion which implies syntax behind names. It needs neither reference nor music. Rhythm is enough.

Or take the following, which can be spoken to the rhythm of "Old MacDonald Had a Farm":

"Oh but Yes But," by Buddy Burniske

> Oh but yes but still but rather
> Yes oh yes oh yes
> And no but still but rather no
> Yes oh yes oh yes
>
> With a no no yet
> And a no no still
> Still a no
> Yet a no
> Always ever no no
> Oh but yes but still but rather
> Yes oh yes oh yes

Whether this could be said to signify indecision, to be a simple exercise on qualifying adverbs, or to imply a more important meditation on the Everlasting Nay or the Everlasting Yea, isn't clear. But certainly it puts attention on *yes*, on *no*, and on all the degrees of gradation between. And it does not need the tune of "Old MacDonald," only the rhythmic pattern.

Both of these examples have simple, linear rhythm. But the first, since it is set to the rhythm of "Frere Jacques," which is a round, has the capability of complication. That is, it can be said in a speaking chorus, "Gertrude Stein" following "John Dos Passos" and "Lawrence Ferlinghetti" highlighted, until the first part consolidates with "Valentine, Please be Mine," all the other three parts following along behind. Speaking choruses, since they involve words, therefore reference, must be modulated, so that whatever motif needs highlighting can be heard above the other parts.

The distinction between simple, one-part, or linear rhythm patterns and speaking choruses or chorales is one of scale. Variation and complexity have far greater emotional potential when chanted by a speaking chorus, and the impact of a single word can resonate.

The following exercises are divided between those that use melody and harmony, and those that do not. They are calculated to put attention on words as parts of speech, on verb conjugations, on the position of qualifying phrases, on sentence structure, sentence permutations, on nonsense or code words, and on abstract sound.

Exercise 45: Verb-Conjugation Oratorio with Music

Purpose: To place attention on verb conjugation. To isolate, strip, and abstract a verb to appreciate myriad possibilities of usage.

Background: Check all the aspects of a verb:

Person
Number
Tense
Voice
Mood
Type

1. Choose a movement of a symphony or some other instrumental music.

2. Choose three or four verbs which, used in combination, can develop a thought or idea, or which used, in contrast, can create a dynamic argument or dialogue.

3. Design an oratorio for speaking chorus with three or more parts to be spoken by people or groups, solos or choruses. *Use subject and verb only.* But you may vary the conjugation, tense, voice, and mood, and you may use whatever helping verbs you need.

4. Suggestions: Common verbs are the most powerful, and conjure common verbs with an opposite meaning. Be aware of the vowel sound of the verbs, and the number of syllables. Be sure the choral dialogue has a message, plot, or dynamic. Think of the parts of the chorus as voices of people in a play who are arguing or inveighing against one another. Or the chorus may act as commentator, as in Greek drama. Or as jury. Or as a crowd of accusers, etc.

5. The words should begin with the beginning of the movement and conclude at a suitable end point within the movement, or at the end of the movement.

Exercise 46: Miscellaneous Refrain Chorus with Music

Purpose: To place attention on stray themes, referential words, and nonsense which, by virtue of their conjunction, express a statement.

1. Choose a movement of a symphony or some other instrumental music.

2. Write down the sentence refrains, phrases, words, and nonsense expressions. These will form the basis for parts.

3. Design a speaking chorus for three or more parts (people or groups, solos or choruses). Use the refrain in any combination so that they develop as the music develops to express some unified message.

4. The words should begin with the beginning of the piece and conclude at a suitable end point within, or at the musical ending.

Exercise 47: Sentence Structure Chorale without Music

Purpose: Using the rhythmic pattern of a very familiar piece of music to place attention on a sentence structure and the syntax of modifying phrases.

Using the rhythmic pattern of a very familiar piece of music to place attention on names.

1. Choose the rhythmic pattern of a familiar or cliché piece of music. Examples: Hallelujah Chorus, Beethoven's Fifth, "Battle Hymn of the Republic," etc.

No music will be played. The rhythm alone will suffice as the rhythmic basis for the chorus.

2. Choose a sentence with a rhythm that will fit into the familiar musical rhythm. The sentence should contain two or more qualifying phrases. Change the position of the phrases into different orders. Repeat the changes.

3. Design a speaking chorus for three or more parts (people or groups, solos or choruses).

Example:

"Automobile Chorus" based on the "Hallelujah Chorus"

> Voice: Lisa rode in the car. She was my sister. I loved her.
> Lisa, my sister, whom I loved, rode in the car.
> Lisa (my sister, whom I loved) rode in the car
> Lisa—my sister; I loved her—rode in the car.
>
> A, B, C, D): (A, B) Lisa,
> (C, D) my sister. Whom I loved
> A, B, C, D): My sister, My sister. She rode in the car.
> A, B): Lisa,
> C, D) my sister   Whom I loved   A) I loved her I loved her
> B) My sister My sister
> C, D): In the auto   Whom I loved   C) Lisa Lisa
> D) She rode in She rode in
> A, B, C, D): She rode in the car.
> A, B, C, D): For the Ford auto mo bile yes reigneth
> Chorus A): I loved her My sister (Repeat)
> Chorus B): Automobile She rode in (Repeat)
> A, B, C, D): And the Toyota mo bile yes reigneth
> Chorus A): Automobile She rode in (Repeat)
> Chorus B): I loved her Toyota (Repeat)
> A, B, C, D): And the Mercedes Benz also reigneth
> Chorus A): Automobile (Repeat)
> Chorus B): Toyota I love her My sister (Repeat)
> Chorus C): Mercedes Toyota Mercedes (Repeat)
> A, B): My sister rode in the Ford

C, D): And she rode in the Toy ot
A, B): a and she rode
C, D): She rode in the Ford
A, B): And yes she rode
Chorus A): For she is Lis a
Chorus B): My sister my sis ter
Chorus A): I love her Lis a
Chorus B): My sister my sis ter
Chorus A): And she shall ride
Chorus B): Automobile Automobile
Chorus A): And she shall ride
Chorus B): Toyota Toyota
Chorus A): And she shall ride
Chorus B):   Mercedes Mercedes
Chorus A): Whom I love
Chorus B):   Whom I love
All): Whom I love Repeat (4 times)
Chorus B):   Automobile Automobile (Repeat)
Chorus C):   Toyota Toyota   (Repeat)
Chorus D):   Mercedes Mercedes   (Repeat)
Chorus E):   I love it I love it (Repeat)
Chorus F):   My sister My sister (Repeat)
All): Au to mo bile whom I love

Logic: Generalization through rhythmic listing

Part of the value of the "Automobile Chorus" was the enumeration of the brand names of automobiles, particularly those of three syllables.

Rhythmic accentuation using words in choral form combines reference with rhythm. But the intellect forms connections out of the referential material beyond the realm of the rhythm. The rhythm acts to "point out," to "pay attention." Once the mind pays attention a second step occurs. Unstated implication.

Such a demonstration in rhythmic form amounts to a tour de force. Ernst Toch, the Austrian composer, who believed strongly that artists form an involuntary link in an evolutionary chain, and that the artistic process, like the biological one, is organic, experimented with choral and dramatic pieces. He wrote a speaking chorale called the "Geographical Fuguei" in *Gesprochene Musik* in 1930, in which he used the names of geographical places of two, three, and four syllables. He organized them with pure, rhythmic counterpoint. The words were:

Two syllable	Three syllable	Four syllable
Tibet	Canada	Mississippi
Poland	Malaga	Titicaca
China	Brindisi	Honolulu
Denmark	Trinidad	Massachusetts

The effect is funny, a mathematical posing of the obvious until it bursts a seam to a sense of wonder. Over what? Seemingly nothing. But really, over the idea of *category*.

Exercise 48: Category-Example Fugue without Music

Purpose: To place attention on category, subject, type, and species by iterating and reiterating specific names of the category.

1. Choose a subject, species, type, or category.

2. Choose the names of specific examples that illustrate the category. Restrict yourself. If it is automobiles, restrict yourself to the names only. If it is animals, restrict yourself to the names. If it is geographical, restrict yourself to geographical names, etc.

3. Separate the names into one-, two-, three-, and four-syllable words.

4. Arrange the names, using augmentation, diminution, and stretto, all the techniques of the fugue form, into at least three or more parts.

Exercise 49: Code-Word Ensemble without Music

Purpose: To demonstrate the rhythms of abstract sounds. To create an ensemble using vowels and consonants in rhythms which hint of the power beyond words.

Consideration: Be aware of the alchemy of vowels, the emotional difference in affect of the short sounds, long, diphthong sounds of *a, e, i, o, u,* and of their doubling.

Also keep in mind the difference in emotion of gutturals, sibilants, aspirants, fricatives, and affricatives, as outlined in chapter 8.

Write a "sound piece" that lasts no less than one minute and no more than three minutes.

1. Invent a "code word" (a word with no referential meaning, easy to say, easy to remember, with assonance and resonance). Though it is pure invention and without meaning, it should sound real. It may be one word, or two in combination.

2. Use the code word as a repetitive refrain that will be the rhythmic basis for two other parts. The code word must fit into a fixed-beat measure.

3. Invent two other parts. They should be contrapuntal nonsense sections to be spoken at the same time and in rhythm with the code word, to be played against it. The timing should be precise. It must not allow rhythmic interpretation, only color interpretation.

4. Write the piece in strict notation, any kind of notation you care to devise. But the rhythm must be so strict it can be performed by any other person.

5. This exercise may resemble a cross between choral speaking and scat. It may even sound like cheerleading.

Example:

"Teeno Kappa," by Mark Meares, Owen Page, and Ed Taylor

Note: Each "Teeno Kappa" set includes two TKs (TKTK)—that is, eight counts for each set, including the two counts of silence that follow.

The beats go: Teeno Kappa Teeno Kappa

> TKTK—TKTK Heyay TKTK Heyay TKTK
> BuFIbu BUBU (repeat three times)
> TKTK
> TEEpekenoslekee (repeat two times) DOT DOT DOT
> SHIKA SAKA TOOKA TEE HEE TOOKA SAKA TEEKA CHEE
> CHEE
> TKTK * TKTK
> Wha do doe run tee (repeat)
> Wha do doe re mee (repeat)
> Wha do soe do mee (repeat)
> TKTK—TKTKOOTKTK BOP BOP BOP
> Heyay
> TKTK—TKTK
> Who Who wallop wow (repeat)

A E I O U (repeat)
Oh A
Oh A
Oh A
U
Wha wha wowlup wu (repeat)
Wham bam I u am (repeat)
Who who wallop wa (repeat)
TKTK—TKTK
Ho Ha OH AH Hee Hee Smeelay YEE AH (repeat)
Reggie Reggae Reggie Smeelay Reggie Reggae O SAY (repeat)
Smeelay Smeelay Olay HayHay Tassah (repeat)
Loolah Holah Holay OOOEE (repeat)
Elaytedah Elayteday OLAY (repeat)
Elaytedah Hop Hop Hoppee
TKTK—TKTK

The Pulse of the Word

Of all humans, only elementary school children are unabashed or unselfconscious enough to be led to the brink of mantra. Beguiled by sound and rhythm, rebels and slaves of adults, they are captured by the idea of silliness as a quality superior to sense. They open themselves to the experience of being grazed by the enigma and fear of the word. They dare to mouth not for sense, but for sound. And although they are as delighted as TV with jingles of fixed beat, they do not shun chanting a disembodied syllable, or a word out of context to explore its peculiar rhythm.

The distinction here is between fixed musical rhythm, and unfixed word rhythm. Inchoate power hovers about the body of a word in the deep well of sound.

In the last exercise, we will compose chants. Just as it would be foolish to deny the reference of a word, so it is foolish to deny that a chant has no relation to the fixed beat of music. But it falls between the two. As novice chanters, we may take a concept (a word, even a syllable) and turn it back and forth in a sound mirror, led, not by the drums of maestro music, but by the sound quaver of its meaning. That is a concept without credibility in our culture, but it may be a better avenue toward the nourishment of our depleted language than anything else.

Exercise 50: The Abstract Chant for Solo and or Chorus without Music

Purpose: To feel and practice the sound vibration of syllable or word with the goal of relating to its referential meaning. *Do not use fixed beat rhythm.*

Choose a combination of sounds. They may be real words, or meaningless syllables.

Improvise a chant. Be guided by the sounds of the syllables.

You may design your piece either for a solo, or for parts. If you compose it for parts, you may have a background chorus against which soloists chant separate words or parts. Or it may be competing choruses chanting in dialogue or recitative.

Goal: If you use code words without referential meaning, or nonsense sounds, the chanting may create intellectual association. But this is not a goal, merely a consequence. Illustration No. 1 is an example.

If you use words with referential meaning, you may explore a resulting intellectual idea. If you do not attempt to "say something" of an intellectual nature, there may be an intellectual implication anyhow, but it will be the pulsation of words that cause this, not the intention. Such a case will illustrate the power of chanting. The composition is the skeleton, not the libretto for the sound to take effect. The first two examples below illustrate this.

Examples: "AE"

> A) A.
> B) A?
> A) A.
> B) <u>A</u>?
> A) <u>A</u>!
> B) *A-B?*
> A) No, A-E.
> B) A-E?
> A) E-I.
> B) *E-I? Yiii!*
> A) Owe you?
> B) *Oh, You …*
> A) I.
> B) *Eh?*

A) *I* owe you.
B) *Oh.*
A) Oh.
B) *I you?*
A) Oh, no. It's …
B) *You you, you yo-yo.*
A) You yo-yo.
B) *I?*
A) You?
B) *You me.*
A) We.
B) Us.
A&B) Them.

"How Chorale I"

Class Choral:

All: (One after another) How

A) How do you do. (Start after third How)
B) Do do voo doo As you would have others.
B) Voo doo unto you
C) I Love You

End Chorale

Finale

We are continually reassessing the shape of our grammar as it changes, and we have traced the phenomena of changes the twentieth century has wrought in language: (1) the splaying out of the sentence; (2) the partitioning of the sentence to phrase; (3) the change in emphasis from major to minor parts of speech. We have practiced the verb, the noun, the syntax of the Two in the convention of the sentence. We have practiced the syntax of the Three in verbals, and the splintering of grammatical modes into the dominion of solitary usage of minor parts of speech through pronoun, adverb, conjunction, and interjection.

Music has offered us an alternative path for a language that betrays the deep inconsistency in our consciousness between knowledge of the vibratory, and the substantive. We have blasted referential meaning through sound. We have practiced imitation and parody, the music of language style. We have undertaken the idea of sound as an invariable, applying mathematical rhythm and musical melody to words and to syntactical process.

We are still novices in the acknowledgment of sound waves, but if our recognition constitutes the first tentative step toward revivifying a language whose syntax feels dead, then let us acknowledge it. For we are in an age of cultural speed-up as radicalizing as walking on the moon.

Gram-O-Rama At A Glance:
A Glossary Of Terms

Accent: Applied emphasis on a syllable or note. In regular rhythm, the accent falls on the first beat of a measure. But interest is generated when rhythms become irregular. When stress (accent) is shifted from its legitimate, expected location, there is a sense of complication, excitement, or daring.

Adjective: A word that modifies or describes a noun. Adjectives may pertain to color, size, shape, taste, sensation, quality, and quantity.

Adverb: A word used to modify a verb, adjective, or other adverb. They normally answer *how long, when, where, how, in what direction*, and *to what degree*. Often they end in—*ly;* but *always, now, quite, too*, and *then* are also adverbs. The adverb "like" was appropriated in the 1960s as the hippie culture's favorite modifier. It became the hipster's mantra. ("*Like*, not now, man, but, *like*, maybe later;" "She said she'd get there, *like*, tomorrow.")

In such a laid-back context, "like" implies a passive-aggressive agenda.

Alliteration: Repetition of an initial sound, usually of a consonant, in two or more words of a phrase or line of poetry. Example: Jack jerked the jellyfish out of Jill's jaws.

Allophone: The subtle distinctions in a letter's pronunciation, given its placement within the context of a word. For instance, note the proximity to long or short vowels and the softer or harsher sound of *k* in the following words: *k*iss, *k*ite, hi*k*e, haiku, *k*iwi.

Anapest beat or meter: UU—UU—UU—Example: *deedee* dum *deedee* dum *deedee* dum.

Augmentation: Increasing the time value in each note of a musical motif, thus extending or changing it.

Beat: Beat refers to the time value of a sound or note. The grouping of beats into equal parts is called a *measure.* The beginning of rhythmic distinction begins with the measure because there is a difference in the force of the beats and the awareness of this difference causes the grouping. Some beats are light; some beats are heavy. In prosody, the basic measurements of beats are known as *iamb, trochee,* *anapest, dactyl,* and *spondee.* Examples of usage: **iambic:** The curfew tolls the knell of parting day; **trochaic:** Tell me not in mournful numbers; **anapest:** And his cohorts were gleaming in purple and gold; **dactylic:** One man unfortunate weary of breath; **spondaic:** Tough luck dumb cluck!

Clause: Whether dependent or independent, a clause contains both noun and verb, subject and action.

Collective Nouns: Collectives are called *venereal nouns* because Venus, worshipped for powers of beauty, love, and fertility was also goddess of the hunt, and standard collectives refer to animals. Archivists of language love them because they give hint of a physical life and thought patterns of long ago. In an era when birds and animals have been removed by technology from close contact with humans, many of us don't know the collective terms that obtained currency in English such as "a troop of hares," "a shrewdness of apes," or "a shoal of fish." Gone from the language is "a leap of leopards" and "a route of wolves." The collective "a drove of kine" is an archaic expression that was once so popular it was considered a cliché.

Conjunction: A word used to connect words, phrases, clauses, and sentences and to show the relationship between the expressions they connect. *Coordinating Conjunctions (and, or, nor, but,* and *yet)* serve as links between events. *Subordinating Conjunctions (although, as, because, if, than, that,* and *while)* introduce condition and cause. *Correlative Conjunctions* are words used in pairs to connect sentence elements of equal grammatical rank: *Both ...and, not only ...but also, either ...or, neither ... nor, as ... as,* and *whether ... or.*

Consonant: Any of the speech sounds produced by stopping and releasing the air stream (p, t, k, d, b, g) or stopping it at one point while it escapes at another (m, n, l, r) or forcing it through a loosely closed or very nasal passage (f, v, s, z, sh, zh, th, h, w, y, j).

Consonant sounds: Consonant sounds are classified by the position of the mouth, tongue, lips, and manner of articulation. There are *voiced* and *unvoiced* consonants. Manners of articulation include: *plosive, fricative, affricative, nasal, lateral,* and *semivowels.* Positions of articulation include:
Bilabial (use of both lips), Labiodental (use of lower lip and upper teeth), Dental (use of tip of the tongue and back part of upper teeth), Aveolar (tip or middle of tongue applied to alveolar ridge), Alveo-palatal (tip or middle of tongue and middle forward section of hard palate), Velar (use of root of tongue and velum or soft

palate), Palatal (middle of tongue and hard palate, but not a common sound in English), and Glottal (the glottis, back of throat and vocal chords).

Copula or copulative verb: Like the intransitive verb, the copula can take no object. Specifically, these are verbs of *essence*. (Example: She *is* an idiot.) In that sentence, "she" isn't *doing* anything to "idiot." She is *being* an idiot.

Counterpoint: A melody accompanying another melody note for note; or the technique of adding a related but independent melody or melodies to a basic melody in order to make a harmonious whole.

Crowned Noun: The relationship of a traditional given name and its historical essence, what it comes to mean, perhaps based on a person's deeds or reputation. Many of the historically elect are "crowned" in our memory by a tag (e.g., Ivan the Terrible, Catharine the Great, Oedipus Rex).

Dactylic beat or meter:—UU—UU—UU; Example: **oom** papa **oom** papa **oom** papa.

Dangling Modifier: Words (participles) or phrases that seem misplaced in a sentence or lacking the clearest grammatical relationship with the part of the sentence they seek to enhance. Dangling modifiers often have a ludicrous impact on sentences: Example: *Running in the snow*, her mittens got lost.

Correction: While running in the snow, she lost her mittens.

Diminution: Shortening the duration of each note in a theme, thus changing it.

Diphthong: Combinations of two vowel sounds: f*ea*r, p*oo*r, *ou*t, av*oi*d, d*oo*r.

Double Negative: Redundant negativity. Often found in informal dialect. Example: It *doesn't* make *no* matter. Triple negative is triple redundancy. Example: It *don't* make *no* *nevermind*. Or, even better: "*Don't* wanna have us *none* of that down-*below zero* weather *no* more."

Duple meter: Duple meter in music corresponds to iambic or trochaic verse. Its flow contains a succession of beats or pulses that fall into a measure of two beats, one strongly accented, the other unaccented. This is a replica of human heartbeat.

Form: Form refers to shape or a method of arrangement. Rules, logical sequence, or a prescribed method often apply to form.

Fugue: A musical composition in which a theme is taken up by the various instruments or voices in succession according to the strict rules of counterpoint.

Gerund: The gerund is formed by adding *-ing* to a verb. It acts as a noun, but shares the nature of the verb. As a noun, it can perform the functions of a noun, be a subject or an object, and be modified by an adjective. ("Blatant *lying* takes gall, even for a blatant liar.") As a verb, it can take an object and be modified by an adverb. ("Blatantly *passing* the buck is the greatest asset a bureaucrat can possess.")

Gibberish: Goofy and sometimes singsong experiments in pure sound. Gibberish employs only *phonological* rules whereas **nonsense** adheres to *syntatic* rules as well. Example of gibberish: "Inty nintytibberty fig, deema dima doma dig."

Grammar: The medium or network of the relationship of words.

Helping Verb: Although simple present and past tenses may be expressed by a one-word verb, all other tenses require a helping verb. You show future tense by adding *will* or *shall* (e.g., You *will* go.); You show present, past, and future perfect tenses with the helping verbs *have, had,* and *will* or *shall have* (e.g., He *will have* gone by the time they arrive.). You use a helping combination formed of the verb *to be* to show continuous action (e.g., I *am* going, I *was* going, I *will be* going.). And it takes helping verbs to make the passive voice, where the subject is acted upon: I *am* hit. The helping verbs *should, would, may, might,* and *could* express different versions of such moods as the conditional or subjunctive.

Iambic meter or beat: U—U—U—(hi ho hi ho hi ho)

Infinitive: Derived from a verb, the infinitive acts as a noun, or as an adjective or adverb. Of all verbals, it is the most abstract. As a noun, it can be used as a subject or object (*To laugh* is a good thing; We were told *to laugh*). Example of an infinitive used as an adjective: "Gretel had found a way *to free* Hansel." (To free modifies "way.") Example of an infinitive used as an adverb: "Hansel was too frightened *to speak*." (To speak qualifies how frightened he is.)

Interjection: An exclamatory word or phrase used independently in sentence. Examples: Ah! Oh! Wow! Damn! Or Alas, Hurrah! Abracadabra.

Intransitive Verb: A verb that does not take an object. Examples: *think, pray, sit, laugh.* You may think thoughts, pray a prayer, or laugh a laugh. You can not sit a seat. None of the above is very good grammar because you cannot think, pray, sit, or laugh anything outside what the verb decrees. (Actually, you can "think a reply," just not say it—we do this all the time when we bite our tongues. Probably hardcore grammarians "pray rules" that can't be broken, too!)

Main Clause (independent clause): A main clause contains both a subject and a predicate and functions as a complete grammatical unit. (We ate.)

Malapropism: Next door to puns are malapropisms. A malapropism is the act or habit of misusing a word so that it appears ridiculous. Malapropisms are in the realm of "found art" rather than intentional, accomplished satire. Usually they stem from ignorance, having nothing to do with language prowess. Examples: "I rode an alligator (elevator) up the Empire State building;" "He's a wealthy typhoon (tycoon)."

Meter: Similar to beat (in music), meter is a recurring rhythmic pattern established by the insistent regularity of similar units of sound.

Modifying Clause (dependent, subordinate clause): A modifying clause is an imitation of the sentence, except that it does not stand alone. It needs a relative pronoun or relative adverb or conjunction to assist it in describing either the main verb of the sentence, or the subject or object. Although it is both descriptive and incomplete, it must also have a subject and a verb ("I ate a roll *that had seeds on top*").

Nominative Absolute: An extinct form of construction derived from Latin and employed by such writers as Cicero and Caesar. It upsets the applecart of superiority of those who are impeccable and can keep their participles from dangling. Example: *The hordes having crowded into the city,* the king issued an edict commanding all units to man the gates. The phrase "the hordes having crowded into the city" stands alone insofar as it does not modify "king." It is distinctly participial and modifies nothing. It has an independent position and an independent authority like a noun's. Nowadays it would be considered more "correct" to write the sentence as follows: "When the hordes had crowded into the city, the king issued an edict commanding all units to man the gates."

Nonsense: The tautological definition of nonsense is the defiance of sense. But nonsense needs a tradition to operate against. The best nonsense is not a linguistics free-for-all. Its rules lie in the area of gradation from the inappropriate through the incongruous to the impossible. When the idea of cause-and-effect is flouted, you are in the world of nonsense. In composition, nonsense differs from gibberish in that nonsense follows both phonological and syntactic rules.

Noun: A noun is the name of a person, place, thing, idea, or state of being.

Onomatopoeia: Words or phrases that fuse sound with meaning or that imitate the sound associated with the object or action involved: *Cock-a-doodle-doo; boom, kerpow, screech, hum.*

Opera: Even more dynamic than the oratorio, the opera contains plot, or the idea of cause. The opera is a play, while the oratorio is a story. It is a realistic presentation in contrast to abstract/religious/emotional dialogue of the oratorio. Dramatic scenes occur and build towards a climax. Music that embodies dramatic moments in an opera are: duet, trio, quartet, aria, chorus, and recitative.

Oratorio: The oratorio is similar to a narrated story. There is usually a narrator with different singers playing (singing) the major parts (characters). In some oratorios there are no characters. Rather there are abstract voices singing attitudes that may be at odds or may be complementary, somewhat in the manner of the Greek chorus, or like responsive readings and chants in Protestant or Catholic churches. In a *story*, as E.M. Forster pointed out, one thing happens, then another, then, another. An oratorio is a musical version.

Parody: The word derives from the Greek *parodia,* meaning a burlesque poem or song. It may be any composition in which the characteristic thoughts or phrases of an author or style of writing (e.g., a government report, religious sermon, scientific analysis) are mimicked and made to appear ridiculous. The purest parody is accomplished by exaggeration of the most serious features, themes, characters, or atmospheres of a writer. Parody usually means taking the sacrosanct to extreme lengths.

Participle: A participle is derived from a verb and acts as an adjective. It is like a verb in that it may be modified by an adverb and take an object. It is like an adjective in that it modifies a substantive and may be modified by an adverb. There are two kinds of participles: present (*laughing*) and past (*laughed*). Do not confuse the present participle with the gerund since they both end with *-ing.* The difference is that the participle will act as an adjective while the gerund will act as a noun (participle: The *laughing* crow flew from its perch; gerund: *Laughing* in the woods is a crow's favorite activity.) Past participles are so far gone into adjectivehood that you can sometimes forget that they derive from verbs. Examples: the *added* ingredient; the *carved* sculpture.

Parts of Speech: There are eight: adjective, adverb, conjunction, interjection, noun, preposition, pronoun, and verb.

Passive Voice: A verb construction that directly changes the subject into an object; it conceals and may even bury the doer and experiencer in a sentence. Use of passive voice is the ultimate objectification, except when the focus is on the person or thing receiving an action. Example of a valid use of passive voice: "Brenda and Romeo were married by Reverend Rogers." Here it is still Brenda and Romeo who dominate the sentence by their importance, not Reverend Rogers.

Permutation: Alteration or rearrangement; any one of the combinations or changes in position that are possible within a group. Noam Chomsky favored the notion that a simple sentence had only eight variations or structures of thought. Example: 1) Jack loves Jill. (Affirmative, active, declarative); 2) Does Jack love Jill? (Affirmative, active, interrogative); 3) Doesn't Jack love Jill? (Negative, active, interrogative); 4) Jack does not love Jill. (Negative, active, declarative); 5) Jill is loved by Jack. (Affirmative, passive, declarative); 6) Is Jill loved by Jack? (Affirmative, passive, interrogative); 7) Isn't Jill loved by Jack? (Negative, passive, interrogative); 8) Jill is not loved by Jack (Negative, passive, declarative)

Phoneme: A basic unit of sound recognizable in any language. Every letter of the alphabet, whether consonant or vowel, may be considered a phoneme.

Phonemics: One of two branches of study (the other being *phonetics*) that examine elements of speech. Phonemics or *phonology* is a study founded on the linguistic unit of the *phoneme*, a basic unit of sound recognizable in any language. Phonemics is basically interested in the meaning of the basic unit of sound.

Phonetics: One of two branches of study (the other being *phonemics)* that examine elements of speech. Phonetics breaks language down into mechanics and acoustics without direct reference to meaning.

Phonetic Symbolism: The unproven theory that certain vowels and consonants mean the same thing in all languages, that there is universal meaning in certain combinations of linguistic units that produce similar sounds.

Phrase: The phrase, unlike the clause, is *not* a mirror image of the sentence (noun plus verb); It has no need of a verb, but it does deal with the noun as object. To assist in objectifying the noun, the phrase often employs a preposition to indicate the position of the object: *near, under, over, by, around, to from,* etc. (She went to the cupboard *beside* the kitchen sink.) Sometimes, instead of a preposition, a phrase uses a verbal for its word of relationship. (*Stalling for time,* she went to the cupboard.)

Plot: A series of events that combine to form a specific outcome. One thing happens, then another, and the events are linked to cause. E.M. Forster gave an example of story as being: "The king died, then the queen died." He gave the contrasting example of plot: "The king died, then the queen died of grief."

Portmanteau words: Lewis Carroll defined them as two meanings packed into one word. (Examples: *slithy* (means "lithe" and "slimy"); *galumph* (means "gallop" and "triumph").

Possessives: Singular and plural nouns and pronouns are the most common possessors; the possessive case of most nouns is usually formed by adding an apostrophe or an apostrophe plus *s* to the end of the word. The preposition *of* can be incorporated in a phrase that also indicates possession (Example: The hat of my mother). The possessive case of singular and plural nouns that do not end in *s* or *z* sounds is formed by adding apostrophe *s* (Example: boy's toys; men's yens). The possessive case of singular nouns ending in *s* or *z* is usually formed by adding apostrophe *s* (Examples: boss's jokes, horse's tail, princess's tresses). If, however, the word is difficult to pronounce (and, clearly, "princess's" feels like a mouthful of peas), one may streamline with the simple apostrophe (Example: princess' tresses). The possessive case of plural nouns ending in an *s* or *z* sound is formed by adding only an apostrophe as the end of the word (Examples: elves' servitude; consumers' debt; zebras' stampede). The possessive form of proper names generally follows the same rules as for regular nouns. The possessive form of Biblical or classical names of two or more syllables and ending in *s* or *es* is usually formed by adding an apostrophe without an *s* (Achilles' heel, Judas' betrayal). The possessive form for the names Jesus and Moses always end with an apostrophe (Jesus', Moses'). The possessive case of indefinite pronouns (anyone, someone, everybody) is formed by adding apostrophe *s* (anyone's, someone's, everybody's); possessive pronouns do not include apostrophes (mine, yours, his, its, hers their). The possessive form of a phrase is formed by adding either an apostrophe *s* or simply an apostrophe after the last word in the phrase, depending on the requirements of that last word. Examples: board of directors' scandal, her mother-in-law's complaints.

Preposition: The preposition is a word used with a noun or substantive object to form a phrase that shows the relation of that object to another word in the sentence. (Examples: Susie sells seashells *by* the seaside; Dr. Pigglethorpe put his wife *on* a diet.)

Pronoun: A pronoun is a part of speech that substitutes for a noun.

Proper Name: A person's given name (e.g., Paul, Mary)

Pun: A pun is a homonym put to a point of wit. The best puns are delivered extemporaneously and with earnestness. The pun of the word pun is the exclamation, "Upon my word!"

Recitative: The musical form nearest to spoken language. It is the direct rendering of speech into a musical line. Its function in opera is to explain or to thrust the action forward. Melodically and harmonically it is crude.

Resonance: Both in language and music, resonance is *theme*. Themes are ideas that connect the particular to the universal.

Rhythm: The correspondence between forms in spatial and temporal realms. When we think of rhythm, we think of patterns of movement, flow, direction, cadence. Heartbeats, ocean waves, birdsong all express rhythm. To utter a word is to enter rhythm. *Repetition is rhythm.* To beat out the word "butter" in percussion as you repeat it is to create a conscious chant whose implications go beyond the referential meaning of "butter." We all know the meaning of butter. As a word, it is trochaic, and therefore in duple meter. Chanting it takes it past the boundaries of its strict definition, lifts it away from pure meaning and towards the realm of music and the abstract.

Scat singing: Jazzy vocal improvisation using meaningless and sometimes humorously suggestive syllables. The singer's amorphous voice appears to reference various sounds of instruments.

Sentence: A sentence is a series of words forming the grammatically complete expression of a single thought. In an ordinary sentence, the subject is named, the verb acts, and the content is observable as if displayed upon a proscenium stage.

Sentence Rhythm: Despite any common vocabulary between grammar (pure meaning) and music, we are always compelled by the rhythms of sentences. Fast and slow, crescendo, diminuendo, pause, density, and rhyme dominate and illuminate the meaning of sentences.

Short words: Words with the rounding quality of vowels tend to suggest shortness: hog, yogurt, bonbon, plump, bomb. Short-*i* sounds in words give them a diminutive quality, too: pimple, pit, pixie, ditty, kitten.

Song: The ultimate unity of words, rhythm, and melody. The reference of words in a song cannot be separated from the music. Every syllable must equal the melodic duration or each note and every stress replicate every musical stress.

Sound Symbolism: Although they can't prove a universal phonetic symbolism, linguists agree that related languages have like sounds. For example, since European languages stem from Indo-European origin, the short *i* sound that indicates smallness is shared by all: *tip* (English), *piccolo* (Italian), *petit* (French), *piddling* (English), *chico* (Spanish), *micro* (Greek), etc. When one language is related to another, there is definite phonetic symbolism. The *g* in German, which may be associated with bigness as in *gross, grossartig,* and *Gott* is related to the English words *great, gigantic, grand, gargantuan,* and *God.*

Spondee: A unit of two equally accented syllables: *kiwi, hotdog, bimbo, yoyo,* and more frequently found in monosyllabic word pairings: *heave ho!*

Spoonerism: A type of nonsense (or slip of the tongue) in which words are transposed. Examples: wailray for "railway;" A and Poo Feed Store for "A and P Food Store."

Story: A narrative based on a series or chain of events. E.M. Forster differentiated between story and plot, suggesting that in *plot,* there was evidence of *cause.* Example of story: "The king died, and then the queen died." Example of plot: "The king died, and then the queen died of grief."

Stretto: In music, the practice of overlapping one theme with another. The beginning note of a motif may be repeated by a second part very shortly after the music has begun. This is what happens in a round like "Three Blind Mice." Many fugues end with this practice.

Style: Style, as it applies to language, is the musical component of verbal expression; it conveys a writer's mode of expression in regards to clearness, effectiveness, beauty, and the like. Although it is possible to discern style in as small a unit of prose as a sentence, it is through larger structures and forms that we recognize it most particularly. Voice and style are related. If style is literary music, voice is the authorial tone of a particular artist. Ezra Pound called style "charged language." The method of achieving it was three-fold: use of imagery; use of sound and rhythm; inducing both of the effects by stimulating associations (intellectual or emotional) that have remained in the receiver's consciousness in relationship to the actual words or word groups employed.

Subtext: When a director of a play tries to give another meaning beyond or below the usual context of a line of dialogue, he refers to his motivational idea as subtext. It may play against the content of a line. Or it may emphasize a contemporary idea in the line. The subtext of Laurence Olivier's movie of *Hamlet,* for instance, was based on the emphatic assumption of an incestuous sexual relationship between Hamlet and his mother.

Syntax: The arrangement of words in a sentence that indicates their relationships.

Tall words: Words that suggest leanness and loftiness by use of tall consonants, their *graphic* appearances like *l* and *t*, and sometimes simply by their sound or meaning. Examples: *lattice, latitude, lily, Illinois, ellipsis, Abraham, intellect.* The word peninsula is a tall word because one thinks of its definition of being a long, lean body of land.

Tautology: Saying the same thing twice; considered a fault of style. Examples: *ascend up, attach together, early beginnings.*

Tempo: Tempo refers to the pace at which a piece is played, the rate of the speed of its beats. Tempo in music affects its emotional impact. Composers give stage directions for tempo such as *allegro, andante*, etc.

Tongue Twister: Extreme alliteration in which the tongue becomes literally twisted and cannot be moved around fast enough for the reciter to pronounce the words properly. Example: I fell on a felon feloniously. Who's the felon—the felon I fell on, or me?

Transitive verb: A verb that acts upon a direct object. (Examples: She stole the idea; he reported her.)

Trochaic beat or meter:—U—U—U; **doo** dee **doo** dee **doo** dee

Types of Sentences: There are three sentence types and each of them convey distinctive musicality: the **declarative** is conclusive and firm; the **interrogative** has the lilt of the inconclusive; the **imperative** rouses; it is a direct order commanding somebody to do something and therefore collapses the distance between the audience and the performance. In the imperative sentence, the performer allows the audience to do only what he or she says.

Varieties of Sentences: Sentences have variety of type, order, and emphasis. Basic sentence types are: simple, compound, complex, and compound-complex. Basic sentence order includes: standard, inverted, interrupted, loose, and periodic. Basic types of emphasis are: parallelism, balance, antithesis, and gradation.

Verb: A verb is a word to denote action or being.

Verbal: A verbal is a word derived from a verb but incapable of substituting for a verb. There are three types of verbals: infinitive, participle, and gerund.

Vocative: The vocative is the noun to whom a call is addressed. In Shakespeare's *Antony and Cleopatra*, Antony says "Oh, Egypt!" referring to Cleopatra. "Maid of

Athens!" Byron cries in his poem about Greece. The vocative case accompanies a request, a call, an address, an injunction, a declaration, or a dictum. The *imperative* is used; since it is the most direct mode of speech, the imperative sentence is closest to poetry.

Vowel: The letters *a, e, i, o,* and *u* are vowels. Vowels are pronounced with air passing in a continuous stream across the pharynx and opened mouth with minimal narrowing or obstruction of speech organs. Compared to English, Hebrew and Arabic are poor in vowel notation. The following sentence contains all the main English vowel sounds: "Who would know aught of art must learn, act, and then take his ease."

Bibliography

Bernstein, Leonard. "The Unanswered Question." *Norton Lectures at Harvard.* Cambridge: Harvard University, 1973. Also on videotape.

Bosman, Leonard. *Meaning and Philosophy of Numbers.* London: Rider, 1932.

Burgess, Anthony. *A Clockwork Orange.* New York: Modern Library, 1968.

Carroll, Lewis. *Alice's Adventures in Wonderland and Through the Looking Glass.* New York: Grosset and Dunlap,1957.

Chekhov, Anton. *The Three Sisters.* London:Virago, 1982.

Chomsky, Noam. *Aspects of the Theory of Syntax.* Cambridge: MIT Press, New Impressions edition, 1969.

Faulkner, William. "Barn Burning." *The Collected Stories of William Faulkner.* London: Chatto and Windus, 1951.

Forster, E.M. *Aspects of the Novel.* San Diego: Harcourt Brace Jovanovich, 1985.

Franklin, Benjamin. *Autobiography.* Boston: Bedford Books of St. Martin's Press, 1993.

Fowles, John. *Daniel Martin.* Boston: Little, Brown, 1977.

Hemingway, Ernest. *A Farewell to Arms.* New York: Scribner, 1957.

Herodotus. *The Histories.* Harmondsworth, Middlesex: Penguin Books, 1954.

Jespersen, Otto. *Growth and Structure of the English Language, 9th edition.* Oxford: B. Blackwell, 1948.

_____. *Essentials of English Grammar.* New York: H.Holt, 1933.

_____. *Language, Its Nature, Development, Origin.* New York: MacMillan, 1949.

Joyce, James. *Finnegan's Wake.* New York: Viking Press, 1939.

Kirshenblatt-Gimblett, Barbara and Sanders, Mary. *Speech Play: Research and Resources for Studying Linguistic Creativity.* Philadelphia: University of Pennsylvania Press, 1976.

Lawrence, D.H. *Fantasia of the Unconscious.* London: W. Heinemann, 1937.

Lear, Edward. *The Complete Nonsense Book.* New York: Dodd, Mead, 1961.

LeGuin, Ursula. *The Wizard of Earthsea.* Berkeley: Parnassus Press, 1968.

McAlmon, Robert and Boyle, Kay. *Being Geniuses Together.* New York: Doubleday, 1965.

Merrill, James. *The Diblos Notebook.* New York: Atheneum, 1965.

The Mother Goose Book. New York: Random House, 1976.

Plato. *The Collected Dialogues of Plato.* Princeton:Princeton University Press, 1961.

Pound, Ezra. *The ABC of Reading.* New Haven: Yale University Press, 1934.

Sewell, Elizabeth. *The Field of Nonsense.* London: Chatto and Windus, 1952.

Shakespeare, William. *The Complete Plays and Poems of William Shakespeare.* Boston, New York: Houghton Mifflin Company, 1942.

Shattuck, Roger. *The Banquet Years.* New York: Harcourt Brace, 1958.

Spengler, Oswald. *The Decline of the West.* New York: Knopf, 1957.

Stein, Gertrude.. *Composition as Explanation.* London: Leonard and Virginia Woolf, Hogarth Press, 1926.

_____. *Last Operas and Plays.* Baltimore: Johns Hopkins University, 1995.

_____. *The Making of Americans.* New York: Harcourt Brace Jovanovich, 1934.

_____ . the film "When This You See, Remember Me." Los Angeles: Meridian Video, l995.

Toch, Ernst.. "Geographical Fugue" in *Gesprochene Musik.* 1930.

Thompson, William Irwin. *Darkness and Scattered Light.* Garden City, New York: Anchor, 1978.

Twain, Mark. *Huckleberry Finn.* New York: Harcourt Brace and World, 1961.

Tzara, Tristan. *Seven Dada Manifestos and Lampisteries.* London: Calder Publications and Flemington Riverrun Press, 1992.

West, Rebecca. *The Meaning of Treason.* New York: Viking, 1995.

Index

About the Author and Editor

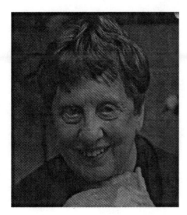

Daphne Athas has written four novels including *Entering Ephesus,* chosen for Time Magazine's 1971 Ten Best List. She is author of non-fiction works *Greece by Prejudice,* a travel-book, *Ding Dong Bell,* a play, *Crumbs for the Bogey Man,* poetry, as well as essays and literary criticism. Her literary and teaching honors include a Pushcart citation, Fulbright and National Endowment of the Arts awards, and the Lifetime Achievement Mentor Award in 2002 from the University of North Carolina at Chapel Hill where she teaches writing.

Marianne B. Gingher is the author of four books including the novel *Bobby Rex's Greatest Hit* and the memoir *A Girl's Life.* She is a longtime teacher at the University of North Carolina at Chapel Hill where she served as director of the Creative Writing Program.

978-0-595-44222-5
0-595-44222-6

Printed in the United States
105231LV00004B/440/A